LIFE REMASTERED

DIVORCES, SURGERY, AND THE SCARS THAT SHAPED ME

ARPIT UPADHYAY

Acknowledgements

I want to start by expressing my heartfelt gratitude to my parents, Brajesh Upadhyay and Vimla Upadhyay, for their unwavering love and selfless support. Your constant encouragement has been my greatest strength.

Secondly, I wish to thank my sisters—Didi, Bikky, Soni, and Sweety and their respective husbands—for always being my protective shield. Your love and care have made all the difference.

To all my dear friends from Amba Smruti (the place where I was born in Mumbai), Our Lady of Nazareth (my school), and work, thank you for the unforgettable memories. From childhood through my teenage years and into my professional life, you have all been a part of some of the best years of my life, and I cherish every moment we've shared.

I am also deeply thankful to my teachers and mentors who have taught me the art of staying composed and steady, especially when things seem uncertain. Your wisdom has been invaluable.

Last but certainly not least, I want to express my gratitude to the universe for giving me the strength to navigate the highs and lows of life. Each challenge has been a stepping stone, guiding me to where I stand today.

I also want to dedicate a special mention to my beloved son, Yash. By the time you get this book, you'll probably be 3 years old, and perhaps 10 when you fully grasp the lessons within these pages. Always remember, Yash, your father wrote this with immense love and care, hoping to guide you even when I'm not by your side. This book is my humble effort to help you understand who your dad truly was and to ensure you always know that I wished the very best for you, buddy. Cheers!

Contents

Contents

Preface

Imagine standing at a crossroads, not once but many times, facing heartbreak, failure, and physical suffering. Life throws its fiercest storms your way, yet somehow, you come out the other side, not merely surviving, but thriving—reclaiming your life with new purpose, joy, and resilience.

This book, *Life Remastered*, is not just a reflection of my personal battles and triumphs. It's a testament to the power of the human spirit to adapt, learn, and grow in the face of life's toughest challenges. From my early years as the youngest of five, growing up under the protection of my family, to the heart-wrenching experiences of two divorces and a life-threatening heart surgery, every step of my journey has taught me how to transform pain into growth.

Throughout these pages, you'll walk alongside me through childhood memories of innocence and curiosity, mischievous adventures with friends, and into the complexity of adulthood where relationships, responsibilities, and health issues began to test my very core. The heart of this book lies in embracing life's contradictions—how you can be fragile yet strong, broken yet whole, and how sometimes, it's the most painful moments that lead you to a place of profound clarity and fulfillment.

Life Remastered is for anyone who's been knocked down by life but knows deep inside that there's something better waiting on the other side. It's a journey from chaos to clarity, from surviving to mastering life. Whether you're struggling through personal trials, navigating complex relationships, or looking for a way to rebuild after hitting rock bottom, this story will inspire you to reclaim your power and live the life of your dreams.

Let's embark on this journey together, as we rise from the ashes of our past and embrace the extraordinary possibilities of our future. Because if I can make life dance to my tune, so can you.

Chapter 1

The Price of Protection

'The rain is falling. Let's make sure we collect most of it,' Manisha Didi, our eldest sibling, took charge, determined to help us save rainwater. She has always been like a mother to me due to our 14-year age gap.

We lived in a small one-room kitchen, often facing water shortages. Rain was our saviour, and Manisha Didi guided us.

Thick clouds gathered that afternoon, followed by the echoes of thunder. We rushed to the terrace with empty containers. Bikky, the second eldest, cautioned us not to run around. Soni, the third eldest watched over me and Kamini, whom we call Sweety, as we were the youngest. Regardless of age, we would address each other by name. The only exception was Manisha Didi. We always made sure to add "Didi" (Sister) or the modern term "Di" (Sis) when addressing her.

Raindrops fell, filling our containers with cool water. Sweety was excited. 'Look how fast it's filling!' she shouted with joy.

I struggled with my tiny container, and Bikky helped.

As our containers filled, my sisters discussed how to use the precious rainwater. Bikky suggested cooking and drinking and Soni wanted some for thirsty plants. Manisha Didi insisted it all go to our home to help our mother.

I innocently said, 'I just want to splash around!'

They laughed, while I joined their laughter, confused. Our containers filled fast. We danced and laughed on the terrace in the pouring rain.

We were a family of seven living in a small apartment.

Let me tell you something about us.

My father came from Uttar Pradesh, the most populated state in India with 75 districts. He completed his B.SC in Zoology, Botany, and Chemistry from Kashi Naresh Government PG College in Gyanpur, Bhadohi district. My parents got married in 1968, a year before my father completed his graduation. Due to the *Gauna* ritual, my mother joined the family a year later. In those days, people married at a very young age, with my father at 21 and my mother at 17.

When my mother left her home, my father was working in Calcutta (now Kolkata) as an office assistant at Benny Industries, a subsidiary of Hindustan Motors. After about four months, he received a job offer in Mumbai, which was known as Bombay back then, as a manager at a hosiery company. Since the textile industry was booming, my father seized the opportunity and moved to Mumbai.

Back then, India was second in the race of growing populations, right after China. However, today, it has surpassed China and is at the top of the chart with a population of 1.4 billion and still rising. My parents contributed to the rising population by adding me to the family after my four sisters. Clearly, they were hoping for a boy or just a little more chaos!

I was born on 28th of July, 1986. Sweety was 2 years older, Soni 6 years, Bikky 9, and Manisha Didi 14. I call myself surrounded by female energy as I was the only brother of four sisters.

My siblings, mother, and I are grateful for his decision to shift to this city because we love living in Mumbai despite its busy and fast-paced life. Our house has since then been at Bhayander, located in the Mumbai Suburban (North of Mumbai). This city offers cosmopolitan diversity, economic opportunities, cultural and entertainment hubs, educational institutions, a coastal lifestyle, and, above all, a sense of security as "this city never sleeps." My father had come to Mumbai in the 1970s when the population was around 6 million, which now has grown to 23 million.

Being the youngest one I was always protected by the elders in my family. The elders used to face the world's battles and share their experiences with the younger ones. In a way, I was happy to be pampered, not knowing the consequences.

It was Makar Sankranti, the kite festival. I was a curious four-year-old, looking in wonder as colourful kites danced high above our apartment window. Some songs were being played while kites were all over the sky and people shouted and laughed and sang songs.

I tugged at my mother's saree, eager. 'Mumma, I want to fly kites too! Can we go to the terrace?'

My mother looked concerned, 'Arpit, you're very young. It's dangerous to fly a kite. The threads are sharp; you might get hurt.'

My face fell as I kept staring at the kites outside. 'But I really want to see how they fly, Mumma.'

Bikky joined in, 'Arpit, maybe when you're a bit older, we can teach you to fly kites safely. For now, it's best to stay inside.'

Soni added, 'Yeah, Arpit. You can watch and learn, and next year, you will be big enough to join us.'

I reluctantly agreed and settled by the window, while my heart craved to be part of the joyful kite flyers on the terrace.

Manisha Didi entered the house and noticed my sadness. 'Arpit, what's wrong?'

I turned to her. 'I want to fly kites, Didi, like everyone else.'

She knelt beside me. 'We understand, Arpit, but you're still very young. We'll show you how to do it safely next time, okay?'

'Promise?' I asked.

'Promise,' she said, pulling my cheeks.

I postponed my kite-flying adventure with their promise that I'd fly the best kite a year later.

However, I heard the same next year … and the next year… and the next year!

I was quite a mischievous child. My curiosity knew no limits, and I always sought out things to take apart to understand how they worked. I vividly recall the time my father bought an incredible remote-controlled car, which was every kid's fantasy, including mine. This car had a surprise – a helicopter hidden in its boot. The first time

I powered it up with the remote, it started roaring like an F1 car. I was already captivated by the sound.

My father told me to press the red button on the remote control. When I did, I was astonished as the helicopter emerged from the car's boot with a "Fire-Fire" sound, like a military commander rallying his troops for action. I was around 5 or 6 years old at that time and had never seen anything like that earlier. I played with it for hours until my mother reminded me to pack my bag for tuition. Even though I went to tuition, my mind was still fixated on how that big helicopter could fit inside the small car's boot.

Once I returned home, armed with my trusty toolkit, which had helped me uncover many secrets in the past. I was curious to investigate the car's boot to unveil its mystery. I managed to open it and retrieve the helicopter, but I had no idea how to put it back. At that moment, my excitement and curiosity turned into fear – fear of how I would explain this to my father, given that it was an expensive car.

However, to my surprise, when he saw the car in pieces, he simply whispered in my ear, 'Don't tell your mother you did this.'

When I was in the fourth grade, our neighbour, Ramesh Uncle, who was a Maharashtrian, had a family with a white female Pomeranian dog named Rinku. One day, they needed to go out, so they asked me to look after Rinku. I played with the dog, and we became familiar with each other.

Dogs have their needs, so I decided to take her for a walk.

'No, you can't,' my mom warned me, 'You are too small to handle Rinku on the streets.'

My mother feared that Rinku might run off.

I didn't listen to her and quietly took Rinku for a walk. Wearing my chappals, I took Rinku and headed downstairs. We lived on the third floor of an apartment building, and Rinku obeyed my command to go slow. I was enjoying the walk until she found other street dogs observing her. Rinku got aggressive and wanted to pounce on them. We were in a narrow gully (alley) with a half-broken manhole. It was covered in a white sheet, and so I couldn't see it.

Rinku pulled me with her as she went after the other dogs, and my right leg slipped into the manhole. I got a deep cut from the broken iron rods. I didn't cry. I was more worried about how to explain this to my mother. I just kept thinking about that.

I managed to get my chappal back on and brought Rinku back home somehow. As I climbed the three flights of stairs, each step had a bloodstain, including the hallway, as my leg kept bleeding.

Soon, my mother sensed something was wrong. Rinku had been repeatedly going to the kitchen and trying to get my mother's attention, indicating that I needed help. But my mother couldn't understand Rinku's gestures.

Rinku became aggressive, pulling my mother's saree, and trying to lead her to me so she could see what happened. I was silently sitting in the bedroom, extremely worried about how to tell my mother about the deep cut on my leg.

When my mother finally came out and saw the bloodstains in the hall and my bleeding leg, she panicked. She called my father, who was on the terrace talking to one of my uncles.

My father rushed down, saw the blood, and also got very worried.

It was a Sunday. Doctors were usually not available on Sundays. He carried me to a rickshaw, and we had to travel 2 kilometers to reach the main hospital to see a doctor.

I ended up with 17 stitches on my right leg. This incident made my mother worry more about my mischievous behaviour, and from that day forward, my family began to protect me even more.

When I grew up a little, the world became more and more curious for me. I wanted to learn and ride a bicycle. I imagined the feeling of wind in my hair as I would peddle down the neighbourhood streets. But there was one person who saw my passion for cycling with concern – my mother.

My mother always saw me as a bundle of energy and mischief. She was worried endlessly for my safety. *This kid is so mischievous,* she thought, *his nature will definitely lead to accidents just like before.* Having witnessed my sisters' scraped knees and bumped elbows, she wanted to protect me from harm.

One Saturday morning, when I was about eight years old, my eyes fell upon a bicycle. I smiled with excitement.

'Mumma, can I go cycling?' I asked, eyes filled with anticipation.

My mother hesitated, her motherly instincts taking over. 'Arpit, you know how worried I get when you're out.'

'But Mumma, I promise I'll be careful. Soni is going to watch over me.'

My mother sighed, torn between my enthusiasm and her concerns. She finally agreed. 'Alright, Arpit, but promise me you'll listen to—'

Manisha Didi interrupted, 'No, Mumma, you can't let him. Remember what happened to Sweety last time she was on a bicycle? And Arpit is way too small. I don't want him to be injured.'

I watched from the window, anxiety in my heart, as other kids peddled away. They rode past the gate and I felt excluded and missed the joy of cycling.

I wished I could pedal away, leaving everything behind, and transform from the notorious little boy, that they thought I was, into a responsible and adventurous cyclist.

I wanted to fly a kite, but I couldn't. Not because I was being restricted but because I was being protected.

I wanted to cycle, but I couldn't. Not because I was being restricted but because I was being protected.

I wanted to go out and play in the absence of my sisters, but I couldn't. Again, not because I was being restricted but because I was being protected.

I understood I was looked after. But, at times, this feeling of protection starts choking you.

Today, things have changed. The older kids don't boss around or shield the younger ones. They know that being born a bit earlier doesn't make them smarter because the world has moved forward. Information is at our fingertips. If we want to search for something, a specific topic or so, we have a smartphone in our hand and we can find whatever we want. There is no restriction on access to knowledge. It is outdated that someone with more experience is automatically smarter than someone younger.

Therefore, the parenting style and the relationships between older and younger siblings have evolved.

We should stop assuming that the younger ones in our family are not mature.

Unknowingly, my family made this assumption when I was younger. It affected my decision-making abilities in my adulthood resulting in disastrous incidents.

Chapter 2

Backbench Legends

Life was an adventure back in my school days. I was known to be one of those who had his seat reserved on the last benches.

Since I was being cared for by my family, I grew up to be careless. I didn't care what was going on in the surroundings. I was living my life free of responsibilities.

I had made good friends during my school days. Raj was one among them.

'Hey Arpit,' Raj said, indicating his mischievous act, 'Watch this!'

He held up a tiny piece of eraser poised between his index finger and thumb. A flick and it sailed across the classroom, hitting his target.

We laughed inwardly. It was that little trick that I had taught him. He had been practicing it for a week, missing his targets, until that day.

We stopped laughing when the target looked at us, trying to find out if we were the ones.

'Smooth, Raj, smooth. He knows it was us,' I said, my head buried in a notebook, pretending it wasn't us.

'At least open your book straight,' Raj said, giggling.

I noticed I was reading—pretending to read—the book upside-down. Just when I was turning the book, a piece of eraser came flying at me from the right side of the class. It was expertly aimed. I was in awe of the precision. This was the moment when I found someone who matched my wavelength.

'Nice shot!' I called out, turning to see the culprit – a grinning boy named Aman, one of our three musketeers.

Aman laughed, 'Thanks! Thought I'd join the ranks of the eraser snipers.'

'Welcome to the club, Aman!' Raj said, pointing at me and laughing, 'You just beat the champ.'

Raj and I quickly became friends with Aman that day, bonding over our out-of-the-discipline acts. However, it was Aman who stayed my friend after our school days too.

As the days passed, we found ourselves in the company of Karan, the first bencher, our third musketeer, who was our regular eraser-sniper target. Even though he excelled academically, the so-called topper of our class, he was surprisingly fun-loving and full of zest.

I had asked Karan if he ever had any fun in life. To which, he replied, 'Guys, I am not a nerd. I do believe in having fun, but only after completing my studies. Though I must say, your pranks are next level.'

Aman grinned mischievously, saying, 'That's the spirit, Karan! One day you will join our group full-time. We are going to create epic memories.'

We did create epic memories!

From prank-calling our teachers to orchestrating classroom disruptions, we didn't leave a stone unturned.

One day as the school ended, we decided to turn the school corridors into a makeshift racetrack. We sprinted down the halls, laughing all along, chasing each other.

Raj shouted, 'To the finish line, everyone!'

The vice-principal, who usually gave us stern warnings, couldn't help but smile at our infectious energy.

'These kids,' she expressed, shaking her head, smiling.

Our adventures were never limited to school premises. On our way home, we explored every road and street. We stopped by a railway track, sitting on the cement sheets nearby.

'Who would have thought that the troublemakers of school would sit quietly, observing the trains, doing nothing, saying nothing,' Karan said, looking at the Churchgate train passing by.

I took a sigh. 'Guys, when we go to the different colleges, things are going to change.'

'But we will stay in touch, right? No matter what,' Raj said.

'Absolutely. We'll always be the mischief-makers, no matter where we are,' Aman said.

I had heard how my sisters talk about finding new friends in college. I prayed that day to have these three in my life forever, wherever I go.

The eraser pranks, the library hideouts, the railway track talks – with these three, who were the first ones who taught me what friendship is.

One of the best days in school was picnic day.

I still remember those nights before our school picnics. I was so thrilled that I couldn't sleep. Butterflies swarmed in my stomach.

Usually, my mom had to rush me out of bed. However, the morning of the picnic was different. My mom didn't have to wake me up, which was a surprise because she usually had to.

She just smiled and said, 'I wish you treated your daily school as a picnic too.'

I chuckled.

My mom had a special picnic menu. She was my perfect picnic chef. She would make these amazing *Aaloo Parathas*, you know, stuffed mashed potato in Indian flatbread. There was also *Tutty-Fruity* bread and some crispy potato wafers. It made my picnic day extra special.

'I have to literally push you out to go to school,' my mother innocently said, making parathas in the kitchen.

Not on my picnic days though.

I grabbed my backpack on my own, my heart, soul, and mind in the moment, and hopped onto the bus with my friends. We just couldn't wait to reach. I had decided I wouldn't share my tiffin but eat all of my friends' dishes. I used to peek into my lunchbox again and again, the aroma of those parathas making my mouth water.

As the driver started the ride, my friend Raj said, 'I had been waiting for this moment for weeks.'

'Me too!' I replied, grinning. 'My mom packed these amazing parathas.'

I immediately regretted saying it.

Aman jumped to our conversation. 'You are lucky, Arpit. My mom packed sandwiches again.'

'But I won't give you my parathas. Mom specially made this for me,' I said, trying to defend my food.

Our destination was Essel World, an amusement park located in Gorai (Northwest of Mumbai), about 15 kilometres from my place.

'I have been there before with my parents. It's a lovely place,' Supriya said.

'I have heard that the best part is the rides,' Deepa said.

'Especially Rainbow and Enterprise!' Mittal said.

'I love the Alibaba Adventure Mirror Maze,' Sneha said.

Mirror Maze, Thunder, Enterprise, Rainbow, or the Dashing Cars, I wanted to try them all. I wanted to take all those rides that were thrilling and just a little bit scary – the perfect combination.

We arrived at the park, and our teachers made us wait to do a headcount of all the kids before we could march inside.

Raj impatiently said, 'Come on, madam! Finish counting so we can run to the rides!'

'Yeah, we don't want to waste a second,' Aman said.

Our teachers finally gave us the green light, and we ran towards our favourite rides.

I headed straight for the Dashing Cars. The thrill of those rides was unbeatable. We spun, twirled, and raced, screaming and laughing.

Deepa shouted, 'This is awesome!'

I found Raj, Aman, and Karan in between my rides, as we all were in different buses on our way. However, I spent less time with my friends and more with the rides.

I would anyway see them later, but I won't see the rides tomorrow, I thought.

When I was done with all the adventures, I decided to ride all my favourite rides once again. I ate snacks between rides, enjoying the food my mom had packed.

I was so disappointed to see the sun setting that day. We reluctantly made our way back to the bus, tired but happy.

'I wish every day could be like this,' Raj said.

'Yeah, no classes, just fun and rides,' Aman said.

'And Mom's parathas!' I agreed.

When I got home, I ran to my mom and hugged her tightly. 'Mumma, today was the best day ever!'

Tousling my hair, she smiled. 'I am glad you had fun, beta. My parathas must have given you the energy for all those rides.'

I grinned. 'Picnic and your parathas are the best combination, Mumma.'

My sisters were partly right. When my friends and I got separated in different colleges, we lost touch and made new friends.

We had entered a world with fewer restrictions. It was a completely new experience, unlike anything I had known before.

In college, we had the freedom to make choices. I saw students openly smoking after classes, and some even chose to skip college to go on treks to a nearby place called *Chinchoti* to enjoy the 125-foot magnificent waterfall. Very few knew the path that passed through the *Tungareshwar* jungle, which my colleagues used to take almost every time.

I was still that curious kid who was eager to try new things. One day, I decided to smoke, wanting to see what it felt like. I started with mouth fagging, where you don't inhale the smoke into your lungs. It was more of an experiment than a regular habit, and I didn't do it often.

I recall a conversation with a friend, who was a regular smoker. He said, 'Arpit, why don't you try taking a proper drag? You're missing out on the real experience.'

'I don't know, yaar.' I hesitated. 'I'm not sure if it's a good idea.'

'It's your choice, mate,' another friend said. 'But if you do decide to try it, be responsible and know the risks.'

I took a moment to think if I should try or not. I wanted to explore and discover, but I also knew the dangers of smoking. I decided to stick with mouth fagging, not wanting to go deeper into that habit.

As the days in college went by, I focused more on my studies. My interests changed too. I met people from different backgrounds, and the new perspectives helped me.

One day, I decided to join my friends in their trek to *Chinchoti*. The beauty of nature was all around us. The lush greenery and the sound of flowing water were breathtaking.

There is so much more to life than smoking or trying to fit in, I thought.

I shared my insight with Sneha, a friend who was also on the trek. She nodded and said, 'You're so right. I wish my dad would understand this.'

Although I had lost touch with all of my school friends, I stayed in contact with two, Aman and Karan.

Testing the time, our friendship was rock-solid. In fact, it grew stronger once we started earning. Three of us lived about 25 kilometres apart. However, no matter how busy we were, we found a way to stay connected.

I was the first among us to buy a car. It was a turning point. Suddenly, we had a reason to meet more often.

We would plan our get-togethers on weekends, typically around 8 pm after work.

Our destination?

Lonavala, the beautiful hill station near Mumbai, was about 120 kilometres away.

Lonavala is undoubtedly a natural beauty, and during the monsoons, it is a paradise with its hot corn and onion fritters – *Corn Bhajji* and *Kaanda Bhajji.*

One of the must-visit spots in Lonavala is Tiger Point. This scenic viewpoint offers stunning views of the surrounding hills and valleys, making it a popular place for tourists to enjoy the breathtaking landscapes. Every time we would be at Lonavala, we wouldn't miss the sunset. At this one time, on the second day of our trip, we were supposed to return early in the morning, but we made sure that we caught the sunrise from Tiger Point. And it's not only us crazy for this spot, but every tourist who arrives in Lonavala. It is the beauty that this place holds.

We just didn't keep the fun to ourselves. We invited others to join us on these long drives too. Some were my colleagues, and some were theirs. We intended to build a huge group, and so we would intentionally hype about the adventure and the delicious food we ate.

Faces changed but the three of us remained constant.

The three musketeers.

We still can't quite figure out how we financially managed these trips. We had just started our careers, earning around ₹22,000 to ₹25,000 a month when we turned backpackers. It surely wasn't much, but we made it work.

One evening, as we drove towards Lonavala, Karan turned to me and said, 'These trips are the best part of our lives.'

Aman nodded in agreement, 'Absolutely! The endless conversations, man. Being with you two is priceless. Oh! I can't forget the songs we play.'

It was something about those 90s music, which was the "Era of Albums." One of the most common songs would be, "Deewana Tera" by Sonu Nigam. That song would be on our list whenever we used to take road trips to Lonavala. It blended perfectly with the town's nature. I remember Aman, Karan and me singing the verse from our hearts, "*Deewana Tera, Tujhe Hi Bulaye. Ye Marzi Teri, Tu Aaye Na Aaye.*"

Even the ones listening to the song driving parallel to us would vibe with us for that particular minute.

The next song on our road-trip list was "Tanha Dil" sung by Shaan, which we were crazy about. It was never the girl we were imagining in this song but finding imaginary happiness (*Dhunde Tujhe Fir Kyu Magar*).

Every word of this lyric is precious today, but it was the only gem back then.

Our lives would have been nothing without the road trips to Lonavala, hot corn and onion fritters, monsoon, and these 90s Album music.

And then there were EDMs of the early 21st century. We used to listen to a lot of EDMs (Electronic Dance Music), like David Guetta, the newly launched Afrojack's songs, and the iconic Pitbull. There were none from our age who wouldn't tune into "One Love" and "Give Me Everything," when played in a club to a car.

We were living our lives, and wanted to pause life forever!

I smiled and said, 'How can you forget *Corn-Bhajji* and *Kanda-Bhajji*.'

'What life is without *Corn-Bhajji* and *Kanda-Bhajji*!' Karan said.

We always made sure that our weekends were filled with adventure. We would drive through scenic routes, singing along to our favourite songs on the radio. The cool breeze and the distant lights of Lonavala welcomed us, knowing we ain't guests anymore.

We didn't need alcohol. Our conversations would flow freely when we sat down to enjoy the *Bhajjis*.

'Man, we have come a long way from those rubber games and school picnics,' Karan said.

'Yes, we have,' Aman said. 'And how Arpit shared his picnic food with no one.'

We laughed looking back at the memory.

I looked at my friends and said, 'Years have passed, but our friendship is still as strong as ever.'

Our outings were not just about fun; they were a chance to recharge, away from the pressures of work and the city. Those long drives and serene landscapes gave us a sense of peace.

Rohan, one of Aman's friends, who had joined us on one of our trips, said, 'You guys are seriously living your life. I so needed this break. Thank you.'

'Be our guest,' Aman said.

Karan, Aman, and I chortled but Rohan stayed quiet, trying to understand why were we laughing noisily.

Clearly, he didn't understand the joke.

"Make yourself at home" and "be our guest" are two different things. Aman joked that he didn't want anyone except the three of us to replace the feeling of home during our trips.

A joke that Rohan didn't understand.

Even though I had started earning and bought a car and was leading a wonderful life, I knew I was free from responsibilities.

My family had taken care of everything. I didn't have to contribute to or do anything since I was the youngest. I turned out to be a carefree and responsibility-free adult.

I thought life was all about earning and spending and travelling and eating. I had no idea how my lack of responsibility and my poor decision-making ability were coming to haunt me soon.

Chapter 3

From Study Desk to Steering Wheel

India's job market was changing in the late 1990s and early 2000s. Rising salaries were up on demand. Western countries started looking at India for IT work because they could find skilled people here. Highlighting, they found people here who were willing to work for less money. Because of this, cities like Bengaluru, Hyderabad, and Mumbai could grow into big IT and customer service hubs for international companies.

I was working at Tech Mahindra, which used to be called 3 Global Services earlier. My job was to sell phone contracts to customers in the UK. A phone that could play different ringtones and browse the internet was new as well as exciting back then. When we compare it with today, Internet costs were much higher then.

Balancing work and studies was not easy for me. After finishing 12th grade, I decided to do distance learning. I felt like I needed to work and help my family financially. My family didn't let me feel too much pressure because my father and sisters were taking care of our basic needs. They have never let me feel the burden, and for that, I was grateful.

One morning, I sat at my study corner with my textbooks, while my dad was getting ready for work.

'Dad, I'll pick up the groceries on my way back from the library,' I called out.

'Sure, son,' he replied, smiling back warmly.

As I left for the library, I remembered my friends, our *Chinchoti* trips through the jungle, and our carefree laughter. Guess, we all have to move on over something in our lives now and then.

At the library, I met Onkar, a college freshman and my friend from school. We settled at a corner table with our books.

Onkar noticed my tiredness and asked, 'You look exhausted, Arpit. College life isn't this tough. Take it easy, man.'

I smiled, not wanting to burden him. 'It's a bit different for me. I'm working part-time to support my family.'

Onkar raised an eyebrow, concerned. 'Isn't that a lot of pressure, dude?'

I took a sigh. 'Not really. My family really supports me. They want me to focus on my studies only. But it's actually me who wants to work. It's kind of a habit now. To work and earn while managing whatever I am doing.'

'How do you manage but?'

I told him my daily routine and I managed both work and studies.

'Dude, you're awesome,' he said, admiring.

A few days later, I had a tough exam. I was exhausted because of the late-night work and I couldn't go through some important notes. I had to sacrifice my sleep and get it all on track in the morning.

As I entered the exam hall, I saw Tina, another distance-learning student.

Tina smiled and whispered, 'Hey, Arpit! I heard you've been working really hard. Need any help?'

I appreciated her offer but declined politely, saying, 'I think I can manage. But it's cool of you to ask. Thanks.'

She smiled, saying, 'All the best for today,' and nodded in understanding.

Despite the exhaustion, I aced the exam. It was all for my family's future, I knew, and my hard work was paying off.

One evening, after finishing work, my father said, 'Come, son, sit here.'

I did as he said, ready for the heart-to-heart conversation.

'Arpit, I want to tell you something,' he began. 'Your sisters and I have been working and it's enough for us. We don't want you to be stressed financially. Focus on your studies, son.'

A pool of tears formed in my eyes. 'Dad, I want to help. It's my responsibility too.'

My father smiled warmly. 'We know, and we appreciate it. But remember, your education is more important than work right now. We're in a much better place with money now. Your sisters are earning too. We together manage the expenses. Take my advice, focus more on your studies.'

Although I was relieved and grateful, I didn't quit my job. I didn't want to break the habit. Also, I didn't want to ask my father and sisters for money as I felt responsible. My family's support meant that I didn't have to bear the load. In fact, most of what I was earning was spent managing my lifestyle.

I have been fascinated by cars since my father gifted me a collection of "Hot Wheel" cars. Owning a real car has been all over my young mind ever since. Two years into my working life, that dream became a reality when I purchased a used Ford Ikon, one of the most iconic sedans of its time, although not the most fuel-efficient choice.

The feeling of sitting behind the wheel of my very own car was beyond words. I was over the moon. There was just one little twist to the story – I didn't know how to drive!

When my family saw my newly acquired black beauty, the "Black Panther", they were as happy. It was a family favourite.

Then, out of the blue, my father said, 'Let's go and surprise Manisha.'

Manisha Didi was married and she lived a bit far from our place. My heart skipped a beat because I hadn't confessed to my father that I didn't know how to drive yet. Panicked, I tried to think of a way to change the topic and avoid embarrassment. Just when things were looking dire, I spotted one of my father's friends approaching us.

Seize the opportunity, I thought.

'Papa, we can go for a drive later. You should catch up with your friend now,' I quickly suggested.

Thankfully, my father agreed.

Phew, that was a close call, I sighed.

As soon as my father left with his friend, I jumped into action. I knew I wouldn't be able to defend the next time. I hopped into the driver's seat, contemplating how on earth I was going to learn to drive. I closed my eyes for a moment and recalled all the car games I had played over the years – games like Taxi Sim, NFS, and Driving School. I carefully engaged the first gear, pressing the clutch pedal all the way down and gradually releasing it while gently pressing the accelerator. My focus was locked on a parking lot pillar to avoid any disasters. After seven nerve-wracking attempts, I finally managed to get the car to inch forward.

Now, the big challenge awaited – making a 90-degree right turn to exit the parking lot without causing any damage. I was so concentrated on mastering the clutch and accelerator that I forgot to straighten the steering wheel after the turn.

The result?

I ended up scraping the side of the car against the pillar to the right!

There were clear scratches on the driver's side door. I felt sorry for my Black Panther. I decided to take things extremely slow this time. I painstakingly maneuvered the car out of the parking lot and into the society compound, where I intended to practice clutch control, turning, and reversing.

Over the next two days, I spent countless hours in the driver's seat. The practice gradually built my confidence. I practiced the clutch-to-accelerator ratio and learned how to take turns and reverse. By the end of those two days, I was about 80% confident.

I believed I could drive.

The day came when I decided to take my parents to Manisha Didi's house. I did it without revealing to them that I had just learned to drive. I knew that if my mother discovered my recent crash course in driving, she would worry, and I would be barred from practicing until I signed up for a professional motor training school.

As I carefully drove to Manisha Didi's house with my family onboard, I looked in the rear-view mirror to see my parents laugh. I smiled at peace that day. I had a sense that we had come a long way from daily struggles to a good life.

I wanted more and better for my family.

On the seventh day of my driving adventure, I was bubbling with excitement. I picked up my phone and dialed two familiar numbers – my school friends Karan and Aman. Our destination was set, the most happening place in Mumbai – Marine Drive.

It had been nearly two years since we had last met. Parking the car, I was grinning from ear to ear. The Black Panther gleamed under the sunlight, waiting to impress my friends.

When Karan and Aman arrived, their eyes widened in pleasant surprise. 'Is this really your car?' Aman asked, almost incredulous.

I nodded proudly. 'Yes, it's mine! Let's hop in. I'll take you for a ride.'

We got into the car, and I could sense their excitement building. Marine Drive, the shimmering sea, the arc of streetlights, and the Queen's Necklace—as it is called—created an enchanting atmosphere.

Our impromptu meet-ups had turned into a regular affair. Karan and Aman were as eager as I was to explore different parts of Mumbai in the Black Panther. We had seen Mumbai from local trains, and now we were experiencing it from a car.

One evening, as we sat parked near the sea, Karan said, 'You know, this car isn't just a machine; it's a status symbol. You are only 19. You bought it and then learned to drive from scratch and turned it into a means of connection. If not for this Black Panther, we wouldn't have been meeting again and again.'

Although I was only 19 years of age when I bought the car, I knew it was not a big deal. Today, we see founders and co-founders of companies turning into unicorns, nailing in their early 20s, making millions. However, it was huge for my family and my friends. In the first decade of the 21ˢᵗ century, earning opportunities were not as better as it is now.

Aman nodded in agreement. 'And these drives are more than just road trips, mate.'

I looked at my Black Panther. It was never a machine but like a family to me.

I made a lot of good friends during that phase of my life. I was charismatic, dynamic, and full of energy. I was known to be a people's magnet.

I also made a lot of female friends as well but never thought of them as anything more than a friend.

Until I met a girl.

She was from a different religion.

Weeks turned into months, while I continued to balance my studies and work, but now with a lighter heart.

Office work seems stressful, like a loop of endless routine, but, for us, it was quite the opposite. We were a team of ten, close and strong, led by our charismatic team leader, Rahul. We had rewards, recognition, and incentives. We worked hard for the extra benefits but we never compromised on the fun factor.

In no time, we became more than colleagues; we became a family. It's as strange as it sounds in a world where colleagues in the corporate world are known to gossip around and play politics behind your back.

But we were free of it.

It actually started with small gestures like sharing a quick joke over tea breaks. We helped each other through deadlines. Slowly, we started hanging out after office hours.

The best part was the weekend. From house parties where we danced the night away to impromptu trips to Lonavala, Khandala, and Nashik – we were unstoppable. We lived through the hills and vineyards just along with the nightlife of the city.

One Saturday, we decided to head to Lonavala. It was one of the most hilarious adventures I ever had. Packed like sardines in a rented bus, we sang songs at the top of our lungs, competing to see who could come up with the most ridiculous lyrics. Rahul, our ever-supportive leader, even joined in, showcasing his hidden talent for belting out classic Bollywood tunes.

I requested the driver of the bus and decided to take the wheel. I drove it on most days in Lonavala as I was curious to explore this side of the ride. No one doubted my capability to ride a bus as they believed if anyone out of us could do it, it was me. With my cap and sunglasses on, I would ride while the driver sat and enjoyed being rested. However, neither the bus driver nor my 12 colleagues felt that it was my first experience driving a bus, as I was driving with confidence. I believed if I could drive a car, I wouldn't drive a bus as well, and anyway, I was driving it slowly and making sure we were safe.

As we arrived in Lonavala, the misty hills greeted us like an old friend. True they say, it's not the place but people who make it look beautiful. We hiked, tasted local delicacies, and played dumb charades by the bonfire.

Back in the office, we were known as the "notorious" team. Laughter and chitchat echoed through our corner of the floor. Some may have viewed us as a distraction, but the truth was that this bond really helped us with productivity.

One day, as we gathered around for our usual coffee break, Rahul called for a quick group meeting. 'Team, I just received an email from management. They have recognised our outstanding performance last quarter, and they're sending a special award!'

We were excited. It wasn't just about the accolades.

The day of the award ceremony soon arrived. We were eagerly waiting for our moment at the conference. As Rahul received the award on behalf of the team, he spoke from the heart. 'This award is not just for our hard work but for the friendships we have built. This bond has helped to boost our productivity. As a family, I know together we can achieve any targets given by the company.'

We all moved in different directions with time. Our careers took us in different directions. We were all separated by our choices and needs in different companies. However, we never let our friendship die. It was unshaken.

Even today whenever we meet, we talk about our office antics and the trips we had. We enjoyed that phase of our life at best.

The last time we met, Rahul, our ex-team leader and forever friend, had said, 'Boys, you know, it was actually our bond that made an ordinary workplace filled with fun and laughter. I never found people like you in my life.'

Chapter 4

A World of Differences

I had been later working with a healthcare company. In my early days there, when the world started to feel new and full of possibilities, I met Alifa. We both were in a 30-day training module, from where, if selected, we would be permanent employees.

Our story began with a simple "Hello."

I traveled daily from Bhayandar to Malad (suburbs of Mumbai), where my office was located, by car. It was around 15 to 20 kilometers.

I had no idea that someone from my neighborhood would become an important part of my life. Alifa lived just a few minute's drive away from my place.

One evening, while we were signing off our work, she asked me, 'Arpit, can you drop me home today?'

I was a bit hesitant, not letting her know my thoughts. But I agreed. Maybe because I too wanted to drop her.

It never stopped there. I started picking her up from her home in the morning and dropped her back in the evening every single day.

Our conversations started innocently enough, with small talk about the weather and daily routines. But with time, as our connection grew, we shared our life's details, no matter pleasant or not.

One morning, as we drove to the office, Alifa turned to me and said, 'You know, Arpit, it's funny how we live so close, yet we never crossed paths.' She threw her hands in the air, saying, 'And where did we meet? An office far from our homes.'

I smiled and replied, 'Yes, it is. But I'm happy we met, Alifa. Like, I would have enjoyed my own company with the songs playing in my car—'

Before I could complete, she cut me off mid-sentence intending to joke, saying, 'You will end up marrying the Black Panther.'

She laughed her heart out. Shaking my head, I smiled at her innocence.

I looked at her with my I-am-not-joking face and said, 'Let me complete, girl. I said I would have enjoyed my own company with the songs playing in my car, but ...' I stopped speaking, looking at her in the busy traffic, trying to make her curious.

The next mili-second, she asked, 'Hmm … but what?'

'But, with you, it's altogether a different feeling.'

Alifa chuckled and said, 'Likewise. You're great company.'

'Guess, we are a great company working for a great company,' I said and we both laughed.

Our daily little trip continued. And with it, our conversations deepened. We talked about our dreams, our families, and the ups and downs of our lives. We joked about our colleagues and laughed at senseless jokes. As I didn't have much to speak apart from my family, it was she who did the major talking. She shared about her family problems and her past relationship. The more we talked and spent time, the closer we became.

One evening, when I dropped Alifa off at her doorstep, she hesitated for a moment before saying, 'Thanks for always being there to pick me up, Arpit. I am thankful to have a true friend like you in my life.'

I had this vibe that she wanted to share something else but twisted her words. I looked at her and said, 'The pleasure is mine, Alifa. I'm the one who is lucky to have met a person like you.'

Just when I was about to hit the accelerator, she screamed louder enough that I could hear, saying,

'Thanks not only for picking me up or dropping me, but also for being with me.'

The pick-and-drop routine continued for three months, and with it, we became best of friends.

'You know, Arpit, you have become an important part of my life,' Alifa said, her eyes on the rain outside. It was a rare Mumbai rainstorm.

I smiled and replied, 'You're important to me too, Alifa.'

We knew we had started liking each other. However, none of us expressed it. I didn't know her reason, but I had many. I didn't want to think much and go with the flow.

About 8 or 9 months into our friendship, Alifa texted me one night, saying, 'I want to talk to you about something very important.'

I asked her what it was, but she insisted she would speak on the following day in the office. I slept with questions running in my mind.

What is it?

Is she quitting the job?

The next day, when we were on our way to the office, she said something that surprised me. I was literally caught off guard, not expecting what she had said. I thought she wanted to speak about her career but it was something I hadn't thought about at all.

It was a sunny day, almost scorching, much like any other, when she made me park the car on the side of the road, looked me in the eye, and confessed, 'Arpit, I like you a lot, and I want to be in a relationship with you.'

I remember feeling a whirlwind of emotions in my heart, mind, and soul. I had a blank expression on my face.

'I don't know what to say,' I said. 'It's not that I don't like you. I do. But …'

I couldn't complete my sentence. I fought between my comfort with her and what I didn't know about the future. In my heart, where things became complicated, I struggled with the thought, what if our relationship doesn't work out and I lose a friend in her?

Was I ready?

'It's okay. You don't have to answer me now. I understand how difficult it must be for you, as it was for me. I had to tell you after days of thinking about it. Take your time, but be honest with me.'

Over the next couple of days, I fought with my thoughts. I was unsure of how to respond to Alifa's heartfelt confession. I had to figure out my feelings for her. I did like her, but I wasn't sure if it was enough.

I have made some big-time decisions in my professional life, but have struggled to take even the smaller ones in my personal life. I never got the space to explore the ups and downs of emotions. Maybe because I was always protected. Maybe because I was carefree throughout. Maybe I doubted my decision-making ability when it came to my personal life.

One evening, on our way home, I took her for a drive on Ghodbunder Road and stopped at the Hotel Fountain turning.

I had to face my inner turmoil.

I gathered the courage to tell her, 'You know, Alifa, I have thought about it.'

I turned to face her after she looked at me with folded hands, realising I needed to make eye contact to convey what I felt for her.

I looked her in the eyes and said, 'I have grown fond of you too, for who you are. I want to give this a chance. I want to see where this takes us.'

With that simple exchange, we stepped into a new chapter of our lives.

For me, a relationship is not about being fake, something which is quite common around, but about building something meaningful together. I knew if I was in a relationship, I would be genuine and it would lead to marriage, the thoughts of which gave me a headache. Since we were from different backgrounds, there was a battle coming.

I saved those thoughts of battle for tomorrow and focussed on the day at hand.

Alifa and I hung out together more than ever, investing in our relationship. Our daily commutes to the office turned into moments of togetherness. We snuck moments between meetings. We waited for the office hours to finish so that we could see each other.

When we were ready, we felt it was time for us to meet our family members. It started out simply as friends, but it didn't take long for the truth to reveal itself. Our families and friends could see the chemistry between us, the bond that had grown stronger with time.

It wasn't long before the entire office too became aware of our relationship. Our friends, her circle, my sisters – everyone seemed to know about us.

Alifa and I were at Marine Drive that evening, observing the sun disappearing on the horizon. It was beautiful to have a warm, golden glow being cast on us. The sound of the waves was as if they whispered their secrets to the sand. We were observing those waves when she shared her thoughts.

'Arpit,' she began, her voice trembling with a mix of excitement and nervousness, 'Let's get married.'

I knew this day would come. I had to step up and see the reality.

We grew up in separate religions and realised how the world might see us together. We made a choice that may or may not be accepted by society.

There was no other option.

We had to face our families and explain our feelings to them. It was not going to be easy of course. There were storms out there somewhere — maybe even an impending typhoon; we weren't certain just how noisy the sea would be.

I looked at her and said, 'We will make this happen.'

While I believed that my sisters would accept and be supportive of our relationship, I was worried about how my parents would react. I thought it would be a hurdle for them to accept a daughter-in-law from a different religion. The very thought of breaking the news to them weighed heavily on my mind.

On the other side of the coin, I understood that Alifa had her own set of challenges in convincing her parents too.

It of course wasn't going to be an easy trip for us. We were prepared for whatever may come our way. She had me and I had her.

One thing about Alifa that impressed me was her persistence. She just somehow managed to convince me that our life together was going to be great, and although I wasn't emotionally ready for that kind of decision, she really made me believe we would become something.

She felt like a hug of warmth, comforting me with the idea that I don't need to sweat.

I have always considered myself a person who doesn't judge others based on their religion. It's the person's character and values that matter most to me. If I connect with someone on a personal level, their religious background becomes inconsequential. Alifa was someone truly special. She was a simple girl who followed the spiritual path. There was an undeniable connection between us, which grew stronger over time.

Alifa, with a thoughtful look in her eyes, raised the question, 'Arpit, I believe in my religion deeply. Will I be able to continue practicing it when we are together?'

I replied, reassuringly, 'Your beliefs matter to you, and they matter to me too. I have no right to stop you from practicing your religion. As your partner, my role is to support you, just as you will support me.'

India is known for its religious diversity. It's a place where people from various faiths come together. That's the beauty that could be our advantage. I was only worried about how my parents would come to terms with our relationship.

As we were discussing our concerns and doubts, I shared mine too. On a personal note, I had this feeling that marriage would somehow take away my freedom. I grew up in an environment where I never had to make even the smallest decisions. However, here, I had to make a bigger one.

I asked myself again, *are you ready? Will you be able to manage everything?*

I was deeply committed to this relationship, yet at the same time, doubts ruled my mind. I questioned my ability to provide my partner with what she truly deserved, and I wondered if I could wholeheartedly invest in this relationship.

Is it a universal fear for every man to make such a commitment in a relationship?

I cherished certain aspects of my life that I didn't want to give up after marriage, and I expressed these concerns to Alifa.

With a smile, she joked, 'You obviously can't throw your towel on the bed after marriage.'

We both laughed.

Our relationship had unfolded naturally, like a beautiful story written by fate, and we were committed to letting it continue to flow with the same spontaneity that had brought us together.

'Alifa, I think you must meet my sisters first. Their acceptance will make it easier to approach my parents later,' I said, sipping the tasteless coffee made from our office machine.

She smiled warmly and replied, 'I understand. Your sisters are important to you, and I'd love to meet them. But, I am not meeting them because I want to convince them. I am meeting them because I want them to be my sisters too.'

When I came to my desk, Roshni, a colleague-turned-friend, looked at me, beaming with a smile, and said, 'It's cute how you both make time for those two-minute interactions between your office hours to discuss your marriage.'

I couldn't reply to her in words, so I smiled back.

The trip to Alibaug was the turning point. I had the opportunity to get my sisters and Alifa under one roof. They instantly felt the connection.

Sweety said to Alifa, 'You know, we have heard so much about you from Arpit.'

Alifa replied, 'Likewise, Sweety Didi. Arpit has shared a lot about the family too.'

'I hope he shared good stories of us,' Soni said.

'Only the good ones,' Alifa said, clearly lying, giving me a wink and trying to control her smile with those cute dimples of her now on show.

After Alibaug, our meetings with my sisters became more frequent. They developed a genuine bond as Alifa desired. My sisters would always trouble Alifa asking about our relationship. They told her my childhood stories, the bad ones, which I never wanted Alifa to know.

Bikky initiated the topic of talking to our parents. She said, 'Arpit, Alifa, we can see how happy you are together. Don't worry, we will handle our parents.'

I nodded in appreciation and said, 'Thank you, Bikky. We need you all around.'

'We will find the right time to talk to our parents,' Manisha Didi assured.

My sisters planned the coming Sunday to be that D-day. All four of them were married by then and were living in Mumbai. They travelled from their houses, warning their respective husbands to support me if our parents called them for a suggestion.

After lunch, my sisters shared about my relationship with my parents. As expected, they were shocked, and not at all ready to accept. They started questioning and saying what am I doing and why.

Manisha Didi argued first, 'Mom, Dad, we have gotten to know Alifa, and she's a wonderful person. Arpit loves her deeply, and her religion should not come between their happiness.'

My mother expressed her concerns, 'We come from different backgrounds, beta. How can this even happen!'

My father said, 'You knew this wouldn't work out, and still you got into this relationship.'

My mother was not prepared for a situation like this where her son would want to marry a woman from another religion. It came as a shock for her.

I knew it was equally difficult for Alifa to convince her family to meet mine. She was fighting her battle there too.

It was like a series of discussions, which ran for weeks. At times, I spoke to my parents personally. At times, one of my sisters called them and tried to convince them. My brothers-in-law too gave their part to make my parents understand.

Manisha Di once came to our house, fuming. She was determined to take some action. She told our parents, 'Meet her for once. Keep her religion aside and see if she has those values that you want your daughter-in-law to have. If you still feel she doesn't, then I will convince Arpit to back off.'

After multiple discussions, they finally agreed to meet Alifa and her family.

I knew my parents very well. Once they accept someone, they spare no effort to make them feel included. I just had to ensure that Alifa touched their hearts. And then, she would not find parents-in-law, but a father and mother in them.

Chapter 5

Three Weddings, One Love

———— ✦ ————

The atmosphere at Cafe Coffee Day was relaxed, yet there was tension around as our families came together. We had spent six months convincing them to meet. However, the real challenge was to get our parents to accept her.

Alifa and I exchanged nervous looks. We waited for our families to settle down. Since her father was working in Saudi Arabia, he couldn't come. We had decided that we would have him talk to my father over a call after this. We both knew how serious this was – our relationship made us go against what society expected, and now we wanted our families to do the same.

At first, it was uncomfortable. Silence settled in. Both our families struggled to overcome their preconceived ideas. Then, Alifa's mother took the first step. She smiled warmly at my mother and said, 'Our children mean everything to us. We want to understand them better, just like you, I'm sure.'

My mother, always polite in public, smiled back, though she felt distant inside. 'Indeed, our children's happiness is most important.'

As the clock ticked, the awkwardness turned into genuine curiosity. Alifa's sister and Soni discovered a shared interest in photography, which my mother noticed. It wasn't just words; it was the smiles and animated conversations that made the difference.

My father was surprised to learn that Alifa's brother had become a vegan, giving up not only meat and fish but also dairy products, which have significance in our culture.

Slowly, we were having real conversations. Alifa and I shared our dreams and interests, trying to show that we were more than our religious backgrounds. We were open to them about how we felt for each other.

We understood that this meeting wasn't just about us. In India, when two people want to get married, it's not only two people coming together but the entire family.

It was as difficult for Alifa as it was for me. Her father, a devout practitioner of Namaz five times a day, held firm beliefs in his religion, making it a considerable hurdle to have his daughter marry into a wholly different background.

When he first learned about our relationship, he vehemently opposed it, leading to a significant commotion within their household. However, she managed to persuade her father to engage in a video call with me. Following several such video calls with me, he reluctantly agreed to initiate a conversation with my family, particularly my father.

We respected that they needed a common ground to understand and accept. We had to give them that space and time.

We left the cafe with genuine smiles, although doubt still ruled our minds. At that moment, we knew that the unlikely 1% chance of success had taken a small step towards becoming a reality for Alifa and me.

Once we returned home, my sister Manisha Didi wasted no time and asked our parents, 'How did it go?'

'They seemed nice,' my mother replied, instantly putting us at ease. But then, she quickly added, 'But what about our extended family? They might not understand. This could be difficult.'

'Mom, we can't control what others think, but we can choose to support Arpit and Alifa in their relationship,' Bikky said, trying to offer a reassuring perspective.

'But will we manage? How will she manage here?' my father expressed his concerns.

'Mom, Dad, Alifa is an amazing person,' I said. 'Just this once, let's not focus on her background. Let's focus on who she is as a person. If she's not a good person, I won't marry her.'

That night, doubt kept me awake. I was sure Alifa would have been facing the same uncertainty. We didn't know what our families would decide. Alifa and I had concluded that if our families won't agree, we won't go ahead.

However, when we woke up the following morning, everything had changed. Our family had made a surprising decision – they agreed to our union.

We were only a few days away from our wedding. Or rather I say – three weddings.

'You guys are full of life,' one of my colleagues commented knowing my wedding plans.

'Step into my shoes, you'll see,' I said, shaking my head.

'I dream of how you both are making it happen, Arpit,' she said, picturing herself in the oh-how-amazing side of the ground.

Only if she had stepped in my shoes, she would have come to know that it wasn't as easy as it felt.

'Just like eating an ice cream?' I quipped.

She punched my arm, smiling and shaking her head, understanding that her wish wasn't easier than said.

Alifa and I had a different perspective. We were very excited, as well nervous, like two eager birds, ready to take flight but with fluttering hearts. We were supposed to have these mixed feelings within us as we had chosen an unconventional path with the intention to do it right and make everything fall in line.

It was a unique challenge, one that required careful planning. Our families had given us their approval, but we knew that our extended family's decision to attend our wedding and bless us was uncertain.

We were in doubt regarding everyone.

Would this relative attend a Hindu wedding? Would that relative attend a Muslim wedding?

And if they did, how would they react?

Would they be excited? Would they be neutral? Would they create a drama?

Keeping all the thoughts aside, Alifa and I had a single goal in mind – three perfect weddings that would honor both our traditions and our relationship.

The first of our ceremonies would follow the Hindu tradition, a grand affair filled with rituals that had been a part of my family for generations. Alifa and I carefully selected an auspicious date and time, consulting with a priest to ensure everything was just right.

Our parents were supportive, but we had no idea about our relatives. Would they question our decision and be angry or upset?

I hoped that Alifa's relatives would attend the first wedding. But she was sure that they wouldn't.

It was like tending to a garden without knowing if the flowers would ever bloom.

'Arpit, do you think Shobha Aunty will bring her parrot to the Hindu wedding?' Alifa asked, her eyes dancing with mischief.

'Parrot?' I asked, puzzled.

'If that parrot predicts a happy marriage, we're in luck,' she said, making me smile.

As stress tightened its grip, our discussions became the lifeline that pulled us back to happiness.

I couldn't help but tease Alifa. 'You know, this priest, that my parents have chosen, speaks more Sanskrit than I ever knew.'

'Well, I hope he doesn't start testing your knowledge mid-ceremony,' Alifa said, laughing along.

'I think I have to start attending a quick masterclass,' I said and laughed louder.

Next came the Muslim ceremony to think of. When we planned it, I turned out to be the most involved in Alifa's world. I was eager to understand her culture. It was something new to me.

'You understand now why I was so excited for a Hindu wedding,' Alifa said.

It was truly beautiful to realise how Alifa and I were involved in each other's traditions.

Her brother winked at me and said, 'You're a quick learner, Arpit. By the end of this, you'll know more about this culture than I do.'

Looking towards Alifa, pointing at her with my eyes, I said, 'Well, I have got the best teacher.'

But it wasn't all fun and games. We had our share of skeptics too. Her aunt, trying to be serious, said, 'Arpit, you sure you're not just marrying our lovely daughter because she makes a delicious biryani?'

Alifa shot back, "Phuphi (Aunt from the mother's side), trust me, it's our bond that's stronger than any biryani."

I looked at her and grinned. I took it as a casual joke but Alifa told me later that the aunty was taunting us in her own way.

Except for a few, Alifa's entire family took the lead in organising the second function, and I gladly followed.

Alifa's parents, like mine, had their concerns, particularly about how their extended family and friends would react. Most of them already had denied visiting the Hindu wedding, so I also doubted that my relatives would do the same. I left the questions to be answered over time and focused on the plans at hand.

One evening, as we sat planning the date of our third wedding, the legal court ceremony, Alifa confessed, 'I'm starting to worry that I'll trip over my own feet when we exchange vows.'

'Don't worry, I'll be there to catch you, just like I have been all along,' I said.

'You know, this will be the easiest "I do" of all,' she said.

The first wedding was conducted according to the Hindu ritual, as planned. It was a simple and intimate affair. We intentionally kept it low-key, inviting only our immediate family members and a few close friends. My four sisters and their families, along with relatives from both my mother's and father's sides were present. My father had invited two of his closest friends, adding a touch of familiarity to the gathering. I had also invited Karan and Aman, my two best friends, to the wedding.

Alifa's parents, although supportive of our choice to marry as per Hindu traditions, had some trouble due to the strict religious customs of her community.

Not all of her extended family members could attend the ceremony. Alifa and her family had initially reached out to them, but upon receiving declines, they respected their relatives' wishes and didn't push further.

'Should I talk to them?' I had asked Alifa a week earlier, as soon as I got to know that most of her relatives couldn't make it.

'We will seek their blessings in the second wedding,' she said, a bit of angry, a bit of calm.

I didn't request further. I could only handle things that were possible for me. She was anyway right. Those who missed the first wedding will be present at the second wedding.

Although it was low-key, we had transformed a small hall into a charming setting for the ceremony. A Hindu wedding is itself a vibrant and culturally rich celebration. We had decorated a visually stunning and meaningful ambiance for the day.

Every guest who entered the wedding hall could see the path adorned with a beautiful archway known as the *Toran*. It is typically made of marigold flowers, mango leaves, and other colourful elements. *Toran* is often used in Hindu weddings as it symbolises blessings and is believed to ward off evil spirits.

Inside the hall, the guests found an enchanting setup. The stage, where the wedding rituals took place, was the point of attraction. We had it lavishly decorated with draped fabrics, fresh flowers, and ornate backdrops. Bright and contrasting colours were used, as instructed by my sisters, such as red, gold, and green.

'These colours are a sign of prosperity and happiness,' Manisha Didi told her husband, explaining the deep meaning behind the decorations they had made.

We had a Rangoli designed on the floor using powdered dyes, rice, and flower petals. Candles and lamps were strategically placed throughout the hall to create a warm and inviting atmosphere. Diyas, oil lamps as we know them, were used as their flickering light added a touch of romance to the setting.

The Statue of Ganesha, known as the remover of obstacles, was placed right after the entrance to the hall to invoke his blessings and ensure a smooth and successful wedding.

'A wedding is incomplete without His blessings,' my mother said, bowing down to Lord Ganesha.

We tried our best to create an atmosphere of joy, spirituality, and cultural richness that none could forget.

Alifa looked resplendent in a traditional red lehenga. Her outfit was a work of art. The golden embroidery shone in the soft wedding lights. The lehenga gracefully flowed around her, which matched her red choli blouse. Her dupatta had delicate sequins and beads were elegantly draped over her head and shoulders. She wore ornate gold jewellery, including a heavy necklace, earrings, and bangles, which added to her bridal charm.

Sweety knew a Mehndi artist who completed Alifa's bridal look with henna designs on her hands and feet.

On the other side, I had worn a cream-colored sherwani that featured subtle gold accents and embroidery that exuded regal charm. Beneath the sherwani, I wore a simple but stylish kurta. It was paired with churidar pants, which added a touch of tradition. Around my neck, I sported a matching cream-coloured stole and completed my look with a turban.

Surrounded by our loved ones, we walked on the sacred journey of the "Saat Pheres", taking seven rounds around a sacred fire while Vedic mantras filled the air.

As the ceremony continued, Sweety, my sister, always the witty one, leaned over and whispered to me, 'Arpit, you better not trip during these rounds; that would be a memorable start to married life!'

I was happy knowing that we were not only uniting as a couple but also blending our families and cultures in a way that was uniquely ours.

After completing the *pheres*, Alifa's mother, with tears in her eyes, said, 'May your marriage be as eternal as the sacred fire that witnessed this union.'

Alifa and I exchanged smiles, silently promising each other a lifetime of understanding. The first wedding, though simple, was the beginning of our journey as a married couple.

The very next week, Alifa and I celebrated our second wedding, following the Muslim tradition – the *Nikah*.

As guests approached the wedding hall, they found the magnificent entrance adorned that had an exquisite archway called the *Mehrab*, a symbol of the mosque's prayer niche, signifying the spiritual significance of the occasion. It had Arabic calligraphy, verses from the Quran, and was crafted with lush floral arrangements.

Inside the hall, the Mandap was designed with flowing fabrics in rich hues of deep red, royal blue, and gold. Floral arrangements, particularly white roses were placed around the Mandap.

'This is for purity and unity,' Alifa had told me during our preparations.

The graceful chandeliers hung from the ceiling softly illuminating the hall with warm and golden light.

The dining area was equally impressive. Long tables were dressed in elegant linens with patterns that featured geometric designs inspired by Islamic art. Each table boasted centrepieces composed of fragrant flowers.

Guests were seated on plush cushions and low tables. It had something to do with the guests communicating with each other that I had overheard from my father-in-law.

'I didn't ask him what and why about the decorations as I didn't want to feel like I was being interrogative,' I told Alifa.

'Ask me later on, and I'll tell you everything,' she said, bringing our focus to the guests, to whom we had to smile back.

At this wedding, Alifa had worn a stunning cream-coloured gown, while I had donned a traditional sherwani. I had no idea how to describe the attire. I was trying to fit in with whatever they asked of me. We were looking stunning together, and only that made sense.

Following the *Nikah*, we had the *Dawat-e-Dalimah*, also known as the *Walimah*, a joyous feast to celebrate our union.

All of Alifa's family members were part of the *Dawat*, and I was pleasantly surprised to find that none of my family members had declined the invitation. They were all present, blending in and making their presence felt.

'See, didn't I tell you, my parents will take time, but once they accept, they will fight the world for us,' I told Alifa.

In between the celebrations, Karan and Aman, always the jokers, couldn't resist a wisecrack. Karan leaned over and said, 'Arpit, if this means we get to enjoy biryani at every family event from now on, I'm all in.' Even though he was a Brahmin, he used to eat non-veg dishes outside his house.

I laughed, appreciating the humour and the delicious prospect of future family gatherings. Alifa and I exchanged warm glances, knowing that our relationship had brought our families together in a beautiful way.

As per the Muslim tradition, I had to make an affidavit, changing my name to Aamir Sheikh for the duration of the *Nikah*. It was a requirement for the ceremony. Alifa had initially insisted not to go with it, but I didn't want to disappoint her or her family. After all, she had made adjustments for me during the Hindu wedding, and it was only fair that I did the same for her.

The name change was a symbolic gesture, a way to honour her tradition during the wedding itself. I reassured her that I would continue to use my real name officially afterward.

Our second wedding, steeped in Muslim tradition, was beautiful. It ended on a high note.

We ticked another box.

Our third wedding, the court marriage, was the final step in our journey to being officially married. It was a stark contrast to the previous elaborate ceremonies, with only our immediate families present, and no relatives in sight. It was a simple affair, but the significance was immense.

As we stood there, pen in hand, ready to sign the papers, I shared a light-hearted moment with Alifa. 'You were right, this is the easiest "I do" of all.'

'Now that I am with you, you are going to say this for your entire life,' she said, grinning.

That moment at the court was brief but powerful, a perfect beginning to the next chapter of our story.

After the court marriage, Alifa and I began our life together, sharing a home and creating a future as a married couple.

It was difficult to convince our family. We thought it wouldn't work out. But eventually, it did. It was easy to convince ourselves after marriage to stick along. We thought we would make it work.

✦✦

Chapter 6

Fairytale Fades

Two days after our wedding, we planned a family outing. It was a big group of 16 people – Alifa and I, my parents, my four sisters, and their husbands. Sweety's father-in-law too had accompanied. We also had my sisters' cute kids with us – Aditi, Aryan, and Aareeth.

It was more of an unplanned trip with family. Alifa and I had our honeymoon right after the family trip to Jammu and Kashmir. We had contacted a friend's travel agency to plan it out. We could have done it ourselves, but the planning of three weddings had already tired our minds. We needed some break and enjoy ourselves being in the moment, not planning anything.

Our first destination was Lucknow. We started our journey at my uncle's bungalow, where we stayed for two days. It felt like a second home, every corner vibrating with warmth, laughter, and fun.

On day one, we visited Mayawati Park, a large park built by the former Chief Minister of Uttar Pradesh, Smt. Mayawati. It was a nice place to let Alifa bond with her new family. I tried not to take her attention all by myself, letting her interact with the family. But at the same time, I made sure to be beside her, to check if she was comfortable.

While walking in the garden, Sweety slowed down her pace to let me catch up with her. She asked me, 'Arpit, can we pick some flowers for Alifa?'

I smiled and said, 'Of course, pick the prettiest ones.'

Aditi was the most curious of all the kids. She held my finger and asked, 'Mamu, why do they call it Mayawati's garden?'

My father, who knew a lot about home-state history, answered, 'Addu, Mayawati is a famous politician who loved gardens. She built this park when she was the Chief Minister. She named it Mayawati's Park.'

Aditi then asked, 'Nanu, if I build a park, would it be called Aditi's Park?'

We all laughed.

Mother's brother is called "Mama"; in a more loved sense "Mamu". Similarly, the mother's father is called "Nana"; in a more loved sense "Nanu".

Our next stop was the Bara Imambara, a magnificent shrine representing Shia Muslim heritage. Its size amazed us, and as we explored and discussed history and culture.

'This is the painting of a grave of Mirza Asaf ud-Daula, the Nawab of Awadh in the late 18th century,' Alifa told me, pointing at a painting that was under a canopy inside Bara Imambara. I nodded, not understanding clearly what she meant to say. She discerned my blank expression and asked, 'You didn't understand?'

I shook my head to say no.

She brought her finger to the side of the painting where a name was scripted. It was the name of the artist, the painter, who painted this wonderful art. I took a look at it and found out what Alifa meant to say.

'Oh! The artist is Seeta Ram, a Hindu,' I said.

'Yes! He made this masterpiece in the early 19th century.'

It was a way of saying how two religions have come together in the past, this being one of the examples.

A while later, my mother whispered to me, 'Arpit, you and Alifa look so happy together.' I looked at Alifa, who was busy admiring the architecture. My mother laughed and added, 'You are the second luckiest man. Your father is the first.'

Manisha Didi and I exchanged smiles. The love between our parents never faded. And I hoped my bond with Alifa to be the same.

After our delightful visit to Lucknow, we continued to Varanasi, where my cousin lived. Varanasi, the spiritual heart of India, held a special place in my heart. That evening, we witnessed the mesmerising Ganga Aarti ceremony by the sacred Ganges River. The banks were lit with earthern lamps and echoed with the priest's chants all around.

Alifa and I were in awe.

After the ceremony, we took a serene boat ride along the Ganges, with lamps lining the ghats. My father explained the significance of each ghat as we passed by. When we reached the Manikarnika Ghat, we fell into a contemplative silence. It was known for its role in the cycle of life and death.

My cousin, a Varanasi resident, softly said, 'Manikarnika Ghat, where souls find their final journey.'

The sight of funeral pyres and rising smoke left us in silence, witnessing Varanasi's ancient traditions.

Our last stop of the family trip was Gazhipur, my father's hometown.

We could see him getting nostalgic.

We were graciously hosted by my uncle, and due to the cold, we gathered around a bonfire. The warmth contrasted with the 2-degree temperature. As we enjoyed the heat, my aunt served steaming *Chiwda Mattar*, roasted flattened rice and spicy pea snack, and we relished it along with *Aaloo Chokha* and *Litti*, all with the unique flavour of mustard oil. *Aaloo chokha* is made my mashing boiled soft potatoes and mixing chopped chilies, onion, salt and mustard. And it tastes delicious.

It was the last day of our unforgettable 8-day trip. My family wanted to stay for three more days while Alifa and I left for our honeymoon. Since Gazhipur city doesn't have an airport, Alifa and I had to travel back 70 kms to Varanasi for our flight to Srinagar.

As Alifa and I stepped off the plane onto the Srinagar tarmac, we were more than glad to see the breathtaking beauty of Jammu and Kashmir. The air was crisp and carried the fragrance of pine trees, and the distant mountains were dressed in a pristine white snow blanket.

'The honeymoon has begun,' Alifa said, and I was determined to make it unforgettable for both of us.

Dal Lake was our first stop.

I had booked a Shikara ride. We glided through the waters, surrounded by floating gardens and colourful houseboats.

'The atmosphere is so good that I feel like being here forever, relaxing and soaking in the surroundings,' Alifa expressed.

I so agreed with her. It was definitely a place to take a pause on life.

On the second day, we drove towards Gulmarg, a place known for its lush green meadows and clear landscapes.

Here, I had planned a horse ride. We trotted through the meadows. Alifa's laughter was all around. It was a kind of picnic that we shared, lying on the soft grass, gazing at the endless sky, and talking about our future.

The journey continued to Pahalgam, where we explored the Aru Valley and Betaab Valley, named after the Bollywood movie "Betaab" shot there. We hiked through the pine forests, hand in hand, breathing in the crisp mountain air. I underestimated Alifa that she would grow tired, but I was so amazed by her adventurous spirit. She eagerly accepted every challenge the trip presented.

As we reached the halfway point of our honeymoon, Alifa had planned a special evening for us. The entire trip was a surprise for her, but this part was a surprise to me. I had no idea when and what she had planned. I immediately called the travel agency and cancelled our plans for that evening.

Alifa had actually booked a traditional Kashmiri houseboat on the Dal Lake, which was far better than anything anyone could have planned. The boat was an art of woodwork and colourful rugs, an ambiance of sheer luxury. We dined on delectable Wazwan cuisine while listening to traditional Kashmiri music.

In that week that we stayed there, we visited the historic Jama Masjid and Shankaracharya Temple. We shopped through the local market for our families.

Our last day in Jammu and Kashmir arrived all too soon. As we boarded the plane back to Mumbai, I looked at Alifa, who was asleep with a smile on her face.

The beginning of our married life was great. We had made this choice to be together for the understanding we shared.

But … was it enough?

For a while, things were great between us, but after about three months, problems started to arise.

Looking back now, those problems seem small, but they also revealed that our bond alone couldn't sustain a lifelong relationship.

We often argued over little things, and these arguments gradually escalated into heated verbal conflicts, which strained our connection. I tried my ways, which worked at times, but most of the time, it didn't. We struggled to find a compromise.

Over time, this tension grew. We could sense that we had started feeling disconnected from each other.

About three months later, when Alifa and I were out for dinner, she told me, 'Arpit, you know, we're quite different. You're focused on building a stable, traditional life, while I'm more of an adventurous type.

I had planned this dinner on purpose, hoping to fix things between us. We needed to talk openly.

Luckily, we did.

'It used to be exciting when I used to pick you up from your home after work,' I mentioned.

'Yes, and the waiting period, Arpit. We used to wait eagerly for the next day to meet again. But now, everything feels dull when we're together,' she admitted.

I understood what she meant and felt the same way.

'Let's find a way to add some excitement to our lives,' I suggested, suddenly hopeful. I just didn't want to give up on our relationship.

She held my hand and said, 'I genuinely want to be with you for life, without pretending.'

'Same here, Alifa. We will try to make it work,' I assured her.

'Sorry for throwing your laptop last week. I was just frustrated with work and—'

'You don't need to apologise. I understand,' I interrupted, relieved that we were talking.

A few weeks later, we changed jobs because life required us to be more responsible.

The time we used to spend together at the office and during our commute was gone. We met directly in the evening, sometimes at night, and one of us was often late from work.

It felt strange, not just to me but also to her.

We realised that we didn't really know each other. It's different when you meet someone for a few hours, knowing you'll return to your busy life afterward.

Living together 24/7 was a whole new challenge.

'You were my escape from the world, Arpit,' Alifa confessed.

'And now it feels like we are escaping from each other,' I admitted, understanding her completely.

Sitting in the counsellor's office with Alifa, I felt a mixture of hope and trepidation. We had come here with the intention of saving our marriage, of finding a way to clear the growing chasm between us. The counsellor, a kind woman, listened attentively as we spoke out our frustrations and fears.

I looked at Alifa when she was speaking. She cried sharing her part. She had always been so strong, but our recent struggles had taken a toll on her. I wanted desperately to fix things, to see that spark of happiness in her eyes again.

The counsellor offered us advice, tools for better communication, and strategies for solving our conflicts. We nodded, willing to try anything and everything to make this work.

As Alifa spoke, I held her hand, hoping that this professional guidance would be the lifeline we needed.

Weeks passed, and we earnestly tried to implement the counsellor's suggestions. We practiced active listening, scheduled regular date nights, and even attended workshops together. But despite our efforts, something remained missing.

It was getting impossible.

One evening, Alifa and I sat across from each other at home.

We had tried so hard, yet we couldn't escape the cycle. We ended up arguing and hurting each other emotionally. It was a heart-wrenching realisation that the counsellor's methods, while valuable, were not working for the complexities of our relationship.

Alifa looked at me with sadness and acceptance. We knew in that moment that we had given it our all, and yet we couldn't work it out.

We had a conversation about this and decided to live separately, to either stay nuclear or stay together in a different apartment away from my parents. We thought this would help. My parents agreed because they wanted us to resolve our issues. However, even after living apart, we kept disagreeing on almost everything, which further strained our relationship and caused stress and anger.

After many discussions, we realised that our decision to get married was based more on infatuation than true love. So, with mature minds, we sat down to talk and decided to go our separate ways.

We decided to divorce each other!

It was painful, but not devastating. We handled it amicably, which is why we are still friends today.

I was used to having Alifa around, and now she wasn't there. All these battles meant nothing in the end. The fairy tale story crashed.

After my divorce, loneliness entered my life like a dark cloud. I reflected over the thirty-two years of my life. I journeyed through the experiences and choices I had made.

It was my time of self-realisation.

Maturity began to take root within me. I slowly understood that life was no longer the carefree existence I had once enjoyed. I had been suffering because of the person I was. I blamed my poor decision-making ability and carefree attitude.

Only if I had faced things early in my life, I wouldn't have messed this up, I thought.

It was that important moment when seriousness seeped into my being, bringing with it a deeper understanding of life's complexities.

I was leading a life free of responsibilities. I had been protected throughout my life. I was a carefree being. But all of it was gone after my divorce.

The reality was settling in, and my perspective was shifting.

I was no longer the happy-go-lucky person I once was. The bubbly nature in me had died. The divorce had shattered that illusion and replaced it with a deep understanding of the importance of people around me.

During those times, I began to understand the value of having a support system. Family and friends became my pillars of strength, providing the much-needed moral support that guided me through the darkness of divorce. It was in that moment that I truly understood the deep bond and love that existed within these relationships.

Alifa and I had separated just four months before the COVID-19 pandemic hit, and the world went into lockdown. It was a difficult time with the constant stream of bad news and losing some of my extended family members to Covid-19. I had to step up and look beyond my own feelings. Covid-19 seemed even more dangerous in the beginning, and I was extremely worried about my parents, who were over 70 years old.

I gathered the strength to fulfil my responsibilities as a son.

I had to leave the old Arpit and prepare to change myself and become better.

———❖❖———

Chapter 7

Turning Points

During the lockdown, which started just three months after my divorce, I had a lot of time to think. It was like looking back at my life like a movie. I started to see where I made mistakes in my past and what I could have done better.

I felt really numb at first, but then I decided to do something positive. I began meditating and practicing yoga to calm my mind. I also wanted to stay healthy, just like everyone else during the lockdown.

Because of the pandemic, we had to work from home. It was not as intense work as before. Few calls here and there. I had much free time, and I didn't want to waste it on overthinking about what had happened in my life. Instead, I thought about what I could do in the present.

I knew sitting at home and overthinking would simply eat me. I had to take charge.

The currents of life were in flow, and I chose to be the captain of the ship, steering my way towards calm waters through the storms of change.

Since I was stuck at home, I realised how important family is. We had great talks about life. I even asked my parents and sisters for advice about what I could have done better in the past. I didn't mind when they shared my drawbacks. I was open to listening, learning, and change. Their feedback helped me a lot.

'Arpit, if I were in your situation, I would have gone insane,' one of my friends said on the call. 'But you have used this situation to better yourself.'

'Guess, mate, I had two ways. I had to choose the better road,' I replied, smiling.

The divorce did hurt me, although it was mutual, I kept myself awake. I had to maintain the balance of feeling down, hurt, and emotionally drained while focusing on what I could do better from that point onwards.

I also learned new things. I started to edit videos because I saw that social media was becoming important. I enrolled myself in a professional strategic management course from the Indian Institute of Management, Kozhikode. I completed that and got my certificate.

As I became more aware and calm, I noticed that I did better at work, and I got more important tasks.

So, the lockdown made me a better, smarter, and healthier person.

Life had a plan for me, even when I thought I was both, ready and not, to move on after my divorce. I was around 33 years old when my family and I started thinking about getting me married again. So, I signed up on a marriage website and started talking to different girls.

In our country, once you cross 30, people start expecting you to settle down, which means finding a partner and having kids by 31 or 32. The idea is that when you are 30, you have lived half your life, and the other half should be about building a family.

I was 33 and had gone through a divorce, so distant relatives were discussing the importance of me getting married again and settling down to restart my life. After numerous reminders, I reluctantly registered on a matrimonial website.

At the same time, I was pursuing a professional course at IIM, which I was passionate about. I kept ignoring my family and relatives' requests to consider marriage for a long time.

One day, my father firmly told me it was time to think about my personal life. 'Son, some or the other day, you have to think about this. Think, if this is the right time or not. We are ready if you are ready,' he said.

He was calm and understanding.

'I think I am ready, Papa,' I said, looking at the wall behind him.

He knew I was not seeing him eye-to-eye, so he asked again, 'Are you sure, beta?'

Fathers are fathers. I knew if I would have lied, he would have caught me. He simply didn't want to push me for it. I had given his idea a thought. I knew I had to think about moving on some or the other day. On the same note, I believed I would not get married to just anyone. I had taken mental note of the things I wanted in my partner. I had to be really sure before getting married to someone this time, and the process might take some time. I voluntarily decided to go for it.

I looked at my father and said, 'Yes, Papa, I am ready.'

Since he had registered Bikky's profile on matrimonial sites before, he knew a lot about them. He recommended Shaadi.com and Jeevansathi.com, and I updated my profile on these websites.

I sometimes thought that it had only been a year since my divorce, and maybe it wasn't the right time for a new relationship. My divorce had been mutual, without any hard feelings or conflicts. Alifa and I remained friends even after the divorce, so I was mentally stable.

In many cases, divorce can be devastating, and people need time to heal. But for me, it was different. I was focused on self-discovery and needed more time before getting into a new relationship.

However, my family wanted me to settle down because my parents were getting older. My dad was 72, and my mom was 68. They just wanted to see me married and happy, not necessarily having kids. All my four elder sisters were already married, and they didn't want me to be their unmarried child.

They once again sat down with me and tried to understand my perspective, sharing their views without pressure. They suggested other matrimonial sites as the best platform for finding a second marriage, where I could explore multiple options and make the best choice.

Well, they were absolutely right. I had to think it through from their perspective as well as mine.

I asked myself time and again, 'Arpit, are you ready?'

And the answer was always a confident "yes".

During my free time, especially on Sundays, I would browse through profiles, trying to find the right match. I only started conversations when everything felt right.

I was very open and honest in our first phone conversations. I told them everything about my past, my previous relationship, my family, and my belief system.

But life had a different idea. It decided to give me another challenge. It made me realise that even though I thought I was ready, there was more to learn.

It's not like I was talking to many girls. In fact, I had only swiped right on five profiles in months. One of them was Vinee, who appeared to be a combination of what I truly wanted in my partner. She was intelligent as well as spiritual.

Love wasn't an instant spark for me; it was more of an attraction that grew over time. As I looked through her profile, I noticed that her favourite movies were "Jab We Met" and "Vivah", both typical love stories, particularly from a girl's perspective. "Vivah" centred around marriage, invoking the emotions of girls in our generation. I could understand her desires by just looking at her favourite movies.

Her taste in music was something I could relate to, and we had a similar taste. As I explored her profile further, I learned that she was an ISKCON devotee and deeply believed in Krishna. She had even served at an ISKCON temple in Delhi, which created a spiritual connection between us.

Coming from a typical middle-class family, just like me, she seemed grounded and down-to-earth. There were no high-flying traits in her profile; she was a blend of modernity with strong traditional values.

Vinee was a working professional along with being spiritual and intelligent. And I respected her wish to pursue her career after marriage. I really wanted a partner who was career-oriented. My family had a common cause, and I wanted my partner to be part of the same team, grounded with strong fundamentals and values instilled by her parents and family.

Vinee's profile had everything I was looking for in a partner. With the limited information available on her profile, I felt she could be my perfect match. That's why I decided to start a conversation with her.

"Hello," I messaged.

"Hello," she replied.

"Your profile looks really amazing. Something that fits my list," I typed but didn't send.

Something that fits my list was awkward.

"Your profile reflects mine. You seem like a perfect match," I retyped, but didn't send it again.

I gave it a thought.

Was I being too honest?

Yes!

But I had to be who I am. I had to give my honest opinion.

I hit on the send button and waited for her response.

Just a couple of minutes and I had her reply on screen. "I too have gone through your profile. Perfect match, yes."

It began with "hello" to "good mornings and good nights" and then it shifted to some interesting conversations.

Vinee's profile was the fifth and last one for me, and I didn't feel the need to talk to anyone else. After a while, we exchanged numbers and began chatting on WhatsApp.

We shared our past experiences, beliefs, and family stories.

'What is it that you're looking for in your marriage?' I asked.

'Peace,' she said, winning my heart, similar to what I wanted.

She had faced a lot of problems in her previous relationships and we both wanted a smooth marriage with a peaceful life. This shared desire for peace brought us closer.

In a week, we did Kundli Milan, Horoscope Matching, to analyse our compatibility. Although I didn't personally believe in it, she insisted we do it for her family's sake.

We shared our full names, dates of birth, birthplaces, and other necessary information with our respective pandits. We also exchanged this information to let our pandits examine each other's Kundli.

To our surprise, both pandits had a similar view: only 12 out of the 36 Gunas matched, indicating a less strong compatibility score.

When we found our Kundli Milan wasn't a strong match, I asked her if these Kundli results were important to her. She replied that they didn't matter to her personally. It was her parents who insisted on checking the horoscope before proceeding with the marriage proposal.

'Are you sure, Vinee? Because it seemed from your words that your parents are firm believers in this horoscope thing. It's better not to begin if we have trouble ahead,' I expressed my views.

'They are my parents after all. I know how to convince them. Don't worry; this was just a formality. These results don't matter.'

'What about you? Are you okay with this?'

'You know me well, Arpit. I don't believe in horoscope-matching-gone-wrong.'

I agreed to go ahead only when I found her to be okay. Both of us felt that we had a strong connection and our vibes matched. We decided to overlook the horoscope and put our trust in the bond we had built.

Our conversations progressed from messages to calls, and eventually, we started having video calls regularly.

Our Gunas didn't match, but our connection did.

We both shared common experiences from our first marriages. I talked about how Alifa and I had maturely decided to part ways when we realised it was the best choice for us. Vinee, on the other hand, shared how disagreements had caused the end of her first marriage. What united us was the need for peace and understanding in our second marriage.

Vinee also mentioned that she took time to adjust to new people. She worked in Madhya Pradesh while her parents lived in Uttar Pradesh, and I was from Mumbai. Being a central government employee, she worked as a librarian in Kendriya Vidyalaya, making it challenging to secure a transfer to Mumbai. We decided that we would try for her transfer after a year or two. Until then, she would continue to stay there, and I would visit her frequently. She would come to Mumbai once every 3-4 months and stay with my family, assuming we got married.

She didn't want to live with a new family 24/7 and preferred to take her time to feel comfortable. This arrangement provided her the space she needed to open her heart to a new family, and I respected and understood her perspective, given her previous bad experience in her first marriage.

After many phone calls and even a video chat, I introduced her to my family, including my parents and sisters.

The video calls and chats bonded us more with each passing day, but I really wanted to meet her and see her in person before committing to getting married. Just when I was thinking about it, she pitched the idea of us meeting soon.

Chapter 8

A Spiritual Bond and a Train to Lucknow

It had been two weeks into our video calls. We were enjoying this phase of life, learning about each other. I wanted to ask her about meeting face-to-face, but considering the distance and our busy schedules, I refrained.

During one call, Vinee mentioned she was going to her home in Lucknow for a few days to be with her family.

'I'm taking a few days off, Arpit,' she said.

'Is everything okay back home? How is your mom doing?' I asked, expressing concern.

She had previously mentioned her mother's recurring health issues, with either her, her sister, or her father making a point to visit her whenever they could.

'No, everything is fine at home. Mom is doing well. I just wanted a break, and I have got some accumulated paid leave. Maybe it's time to use some,' she said.

'*Can I join you?*' I wanted to ask, but instead, I said, 'That's good. So, how long will this trip be?'

'A week or two. I can't take more time off work. My HR would not be happy,' she said. 'Arpit, I'm taking this leave to go home. But before that, I plan to visit Vrindavan and Gokul.'

'Wow! Two holy places for Krishna's devotees,' I expressed, checking on my phone if the client had responded to my reminder of a meeting we were supposed to have in 15 minutes.

Vinee said she wanted to do a Parikrama, a ritual of moving clockwise around an object of devotion to show reverence. She had a friend in Delhi, a 55-year-old man she had met at the ISKCON temple, who was like a father figure to her. She planned to do Govardhan Parikrama and a few more such rituals with him.

'I had planned it with him a long time ago, but our dates just didn't align. It's better now than being even later,' she said. Then, unexpectedly, she asked me something I hadn't anticipated. 'Anyway, Arpit, I called to ask if it's possible for you to come?'

I did want to say yes, but I needed to check my dates with her. 'Only if it's possible, Arpit. You don't have to cancel your plans—'

'I'm already heading to Indore for work. I can join you directly from there,' I mentioned, double-checking my schedule. I didn't want to cancel the plan before confirming my availability.

'You mean you will join us in Gokul and Vrindavan?' Vinee asked, excitement in her voice.

'I'll have to meet you directly in Delhi, I suppose. The Indore meeting is crucial; I need to be there.'

'I understand. Delhi it is then. Oh, Arpit, I'm so very excited to meet you.'

'Me too!' I replied, noticing that the client had replied, reading for the virtual meeting.

After completing her Parikrama in Gokul and Vrindavan, she returned to Delhi. After all our conversations on calls and video chats, I was excited to finally meet her in person.

I arrived at the airport, checked in at the nearby hotel, and quickly freshened up. Dressed in a grey tee and black jeans, I headed out to meet Vinee.

We had decided to meet at the ISKCON temple in Delhi. I was trying to spot her in the crowd. However, with so many people around, I couldn't find her.

'Am I at the right ISKCON?' I questioned myself.

I knew there were more than five in Delhi. If I had come solely as a Krishna devotee, I wouldn't have minded which temple I was in. But today was different. I wasn't just a Krishna devotee here.

I tried searching for her again, but she was nowhere to be found. Eventually, I gave up and called her.

'Hi, Arpit,' she said, 'Did you arrive?'

'Yes, it's been almost half an hour since I got here. I can't find you. Where are you?'

She said she was inside the temple, right in front of the Radha-Krishna idol.

I realised I must have missed her in excitement and ran back inside the temple to look for her. Finally, I found her at the centre, looking beautiful in a pink Punjabi suit, chanting the "Hare Krishna" mantra.

She was so engrossed in chanting that she didn't look around for me. After a few minutes, she finished her chanting and realised I hadn't found her. She scanned the area, trying to locate me. Our eyes met, and I waved to greet her. She stood up and walked over to join me.

'Hi,' I greeted her formally.

'So, finally, we are meeting,' she acknowledged.

'Yes, finally!' I replied.

We took a stroll around the entire ISKCON temple, and I also met her friend. He was well-built along with being spiritual inside out. He seemed to me a knowledgeable man at his age, who shared his insights and insisted on buying food for us.

We even met the head of the temple and had a spiritual discussion. He complimented me right away, saying my face reflected a positive vibe.

'Thank you, Prabhu ji,' I said.

There's a story when I understood why Krishna devotees call each other "Prabhu ji". During my college days, I used to take spiritual sessions from ISKCON in Juhu, a well popular area in Mumbai where celebrities like Mr. Amitabh Bachchan, one of the greatest actors Bollywood has ever seen, reside. A devotee had asked the question about why every devotee calls each other "Prabhu Ji". The speaker provided an amazing response filled with peace.

'As servants of the Supreme Lord, all living entities are one, but a Vaiṣṇava, because of their natural humility, addresses every other living entity as Prabhu. A Vaiṣṇava sees other servants as advanced enough that there's much to learn from them. Thus, they accept all other devotees of the Lord as Prabhus, Masters. Although everyone is a servant of the Lord, a Vaiṣṇava, due to humility, sees another servant as their master. Understanding of the master begins from an understanding of the spiritual master.

'In Kṛṣṇa consciousness, we address our contemporaries as "Prabhu".'

'What does "Prabhu" mean?' another devotee asked.

'Prabhu means Master. And the real idea is that "You are my master, I am your servant". Just the opposite number. Here, in the material world, everyone wants to place themselves as the master. "I am your master, you are my servant." That is the mentality of material existence. And the spiritual existence means "I am the servant, you are the master".'

I held onto that memory and addressed everyone around me as "Prabhu Ji".

Rajesh, Vinee and I wandered around the temple, with Rajesh being the talkative one. He had visited many ISKCON temples and was a devoted Krishna follower, radiating calm and wisdom.

'By the way, you guys can stay at my place until you're in Delhi,' Rajesh said.

Vinee and I had discussed hotel rooms beforehand. We didn't want to disturb Rajesh's privacy, even though he had insisted we stay with him. Vinee convinced him that she needed some time with me, and he understood.

After our ISKCON visit, we had a meal outside and then headed to our hotel to relax and freshen up before going our separate ways.

I surprised Vinee with a doll that I had bought from Hamleys in our hotel room.

She loved it and said, 'Wow! I like this so much. This is so sweet of you.'

I could tell by her expression that she was genuinely pleased.

'Arpit? I want to tell you something,' she said, her expression turning serious.

I sat beside her, trying to make her feel comfortable to speak her heart out.

She shared a disconcerting revelation about her first marriage.

Her ex-husband, ten years older than her, became pushy about marriage. They initially met on Facebook, and after conversations kept rolling, they met face-to-face. He had started liking her in the first meet-up itself, as per what she expressed. They both were from Lucknow, so when Vinee came back from Delhi to her hometown, she would meet him.

Curious, I asked if she liked him, my heart racing. Understanding your partner's past as a friend is different from when she opens up, triggering feelings of jealousy or concern.

'No! Not at all,' she said.

'Then how did you end up marrying him?' I asked, my eyes on the wall, and my ears all hers.

'I was in Delhi, focusing on my studies, when I got to know that he and his mother had reached my home, asking for marriage.'

'Just like that? Your family didn't say anything?'

'Of course! They said, but not on my behalf. I don't know what magic he cast upon my family that they started liking him. You won't believe what my father told me. He said, "Beta, you are of age, and we are worried about you. This guy is nice. The family is good. For our sake, marry him.'

'And you agreed?'

'Not at first! It took multiple calls from my parents and a whole world of drama.'

'You didn't even like him a bit? Like a bit?' I asked, trying to know more.

She admitted not liking him at all but succumbed to family pressure. Her father thought that the guy was her perfect match.

'He was very much influenced by the fact that my ex-husband's brother used to work in Dubai. They had built properties in Lucknow, and that made my father realise that I would never be in trouble financially if I marry him,' Vinee said.

Her ex-husband told her father that he was a big reputed lawyer in the high court, and convinced him that he would take care of Vinee. Feeling cornered, Vinee reluctantly agreed, though deep down, she said she did not want to marry him.

'This was not it! I knew he was not right for me,' she said, complaints all over her head.

'What happened?' I asked, just *not* wanting to know more about her past.

During her Mehendi ceremony, they argued, and she expressed her desire to stop the marriage. However, relatives discouraged her, citing common arguments in marriage.

'Imagine what my aunty said,' Vinee said and added mimicking her aunt, stating, 'Husband and wife argue, but you shouldn't consider separation for minor reasons.'

I acknowledged her aunt's perspective, yet I believe in opting for an exit when things deteriorate—which is what Vinee eventually chose to do.

Right after her marriage, she found out that her husband would doubt her now and then.

'He would link me up with anyone. Sometimes my school friends. Sometimes college friends. Sometimes my colleagues. I was feeling suffocated with him. It just got worse when these arguments turned into physical abuse.'

I was angry. I could not imagine someone beating her. It was not acceptable. I knew I can't travel in the past and make it right, but I felt helpless for her.

She deserved the love that she never got, I thought.

'I thought he would stop,' Vinee continued, 'I gave him time. I believe people change for the good of their loved ones. But, with him, it got worse and worse. One day, I thought it was enough and I called my father and told him everything.'

Her father instantly went to her home and found marks on his daughter's body. They did a medical test, and when the reports arrived confirming her injuries, they filed an FIR.

Strangely, the husband also filed an FIR, accusing her of multiple affairs.

They finally settled for divorce and got separated.

I felt more and more concerned for her. I wanted to give her the entire world's happiness. She rightfully deserved it after such a messy past.

Our hotel room conversation was so important for me to know about her past. I wanted to stay in the day and wanted to talk to her more but our meeting was supposed to end soon as she had a train to board to Lucknow in the evening, and I had a late-night train to Mumbai. But then, out of the blue, she suggested, 'Why don't you come with me to Lucknow?'

I really wanted to say yes right away, but I pretended to think about it. I didn't want her to know how eager I was to extend our trip together. Moreover, how was it even possible? It would have been too awkward, both for me and for her family. I decided to politely decline her offer.

'Is that even possible?' I asked.

Vinee replied, 'My father is coming from his posting in Odisha. My sister is here too. My whole family will be in Lucknow, Arpit. You must join us. This is the perfect opportunity for me to introduce you to my family.'

She was really excited about the idea.

Her father rarely visited Lucknow as he was a government employee. Her sister, who was an artist training in Bharatanatyam in Mumbai, did visit but not very often. Vinee herself worked in Madhya Pradesh and went home to Lucknow when necessary.

It was actually that rare occasion when her entire family would be together under one roof, once or twice a year. It was the right moment for me to visit with her and get to know her family.

I also saw it as a chance to spend more time with Vinee than originally planned. Chats and video calls are different from being with someone face-to-face. I didn't want to miss this opportunity.

'Are you in?' Vinee asked, keeping her fingers crossed.

'Let's book my ticket,' I replied, and she couldn't contain her excitement, hugging me joyfully.

Before heading to Lucknow, we visited Rajesh at his place. He had prepared coffee for us along with some breadsticks. We engaged in conversations, and I felt comfortable sharing my past, which Vinee patiently listened to. In return, Rajesh shared his own past experiences, including his own divorce.

'It's truly difficult,' he said, 'But even if you don't want to, you have to move on. There is life ahead, and everyone finds a perfect partner for them eventually.'

Vinee then asked, 'What is the wisest advice you would give us?'

She looked at me and then again looked at Rajesh, awaiting his response.

He smiled at the question and, looking at both of us, replied, 'When one is angry, the other has to be silent. You need to understand each other and try to fix things rather than giving up on each other.'

His words were touching, and I mentally noted his advice. As our meeting was coming to an end, Rajesh offered to drop us off at the station.

'No, sir. It's okay. We will manage on our own,' Vinee insisted.

'Look at the time. You won't make it with public transport,' Rajesh stated, leveraging the authority he rightfully held.

We checked the time and realised it was the right call. We quickly finished our coffees and left for the station.

When saying goodbye to Rajesh, I had a feeling that I would meet him again. He was a great person to be around, and I enjoyed his company.

Vinee had her ticket confirmed as she had booked it weeks in advance. I, on the other hand, had to make a Tatkal reservation. Until the chart was prepared, my ticket showed RAC (Reservation Against Cancellation), but luckily, as soon as the chart was presented, my ticket was confirmed as well.

'What's your coach number?' Vinee asked.

'It's B11.'

'Oh! It's too far. Mine is B3. How will we manage?'

'I know what to do,' I said, having encountered similar situations multiple times before. 'Okay, Vinee, just choose one. B3 or B11?'

'Umm … B3! My coach. But why?'

'Just follow me,' I said, as if I were James Bond on a secret mission.

We approached three people in B3 to exchange seats, and thankfully, one person agreed. He was a solo traveler and didn't mind moving to my place.

'Anything for two people traveling together,' he said, and we exchanged smiles of gratitude.

'By the way, what's your name?' I asked.

'Kaushik,' he said.

He was a stranger I met on the train, little did I know I would encounter him again. Thanks to him, Vinee and I could be in the same compartment.

'Now we have the entire journey from Delhi to Lucknow to talk,' Vinee said.

It was during the train journey that we discovered our strong connection. Throughout the journey, we had countless conversations and got to know each other better.

The journey concluded the next day, and we arrived at her place in Lucknow.

I was both excited and nervous to meet her parents.

———◆◆———

Chapter 9

An Incomplete Goodbye

The weather was very cold, and the climate was quite pleasant. I remember it vividly – it was the end of October, precisely the 25th of October, 2020.

We reached around 7 in the morning.

I knew that Vinee's mother had suffered a paralysis attack in the past, affecting her health. So, before getting fresh or taking a rest, I spoke to her mother and then engaged in conversation with Roshni, Vinee's sister. She was 5 years younger than Vinee and looked almost like her.

The four of us had breakfast together, and her father joined us shortly after.

Everything seemed fine, and I was enjoying my time there while getting along with Vinee's family. It appeared they felt the same way about me. I was neither treated as a guest nor as a family member. It was a comfortable middle ground, which suited me well. It made me feel at ease. Being completely ignored might have been off-putting, while too much attention would have made me feel uncomfortable.

While I was in a room, refreshing after the long journey, I overheard noises in the house. I approached the room door and heard Vinee and her mother arguing about something. I couldn't fully understand what they were saying, but it was evident that the discussion involved me, and there was trouble.

'How could you, Vinee, despite knowing all that?' Her mother said.

'Mumma,' Roshni attempted to silence her mother, 'For God's sake! He is in the house. Don't say all this when he is around.'

'I don't know why she does not understand,' Vinee argued.

I felt really uncomfortable. I couldn't bear to listen any further, so I settled myself on the bed, waiting for Vinee to arrive.

A little later, Vinee came to the room, looking irritated and angry.

'Calm down. It's okay. Say what you want to say,' I told her, bracing for the worst.

'I don't think we should move forward, Arpit. This can't work. Our marriage won't work. Please leave right now. My home environment is not good,' she said, holding back tears.

I was perplexed, trying to connect her home environment to our marriage.

What's the sense here?

Denying for this reason didn't make sense to me. I never really understood what transpired that day, but I felt uncomfortable. Perhaps it was a red flag. Perhaps it was a situation that could have been resolved.

My initial plan was to stay with her family for a night and then catch a flight to Mumbai the next day. However, my discomfort that day led me to decide to leave immediately, without even getting proper rest, especially after she insisted I to leave right away.

I packed my few belongings, which I had removed from my bag earlier, and went to speak to her father. 'Uncle, I am leaving. Actually, I have a cousin who wants to meet me, and it's been a while since I have seen them. I will take a flight from there to Mumbai tomorrow,' I explained.

He paused, trying to understand the situation, and replied, 'No, beta. You have come here as our guest, so you must stay. Besides, it's already late in the night, and I won't be able to let you go.'

'I don't want to trouble you and your family, uncle ji,' I said, still standing in front of him, holding my bag.

'It's no trouble, Arpit, son. Please stay here, I insist. Call your cousin and tell them you will meet them at the airport tomorrow,' he insisted.

Although I didn't want to stay, I couldn't refuse him, given the love and respect he showed me.

It was just a matter of one night, I thought.

The following day was quite pleasant. They treated me like one of their own. We woke up, worshiped together, and sang bhajan songs.

Deep down, I felt that they might be thinking I would stay only for a few hours, so they wanted to treat me well and bid me a proper farewell, free from any bad feelings.

After a quick breakfast, I wanted to take a cab to my cousin's place, but Vinee's father insisted on driving me. Vinee didn't even look me in the eye when I was leaving. I declined a few times to her father but eventually gave in to his insistence. He dropped me off at my cousin's place.

I spent a few hours with my cousin and his family, and then I headed back to Mumbai.

I had no expectations after the events in Lucknow, and I didn't want to push the issue, so I refrained from contacting Vinee on my own.

However, she called me once she returned to Madhya Pradesh after her leave ended, which came as a surprise.

I expressed my feelings, 'I still don't understand what all that was about?'

'My family is a bit complicated. Anyway, it was my bad decision to take you to meet them. They met the right person at the wrong time,' Vinee explained.

I wasn't entirely sure of what she meant. 'But why were they behaving so strangely?' I asked.

'Arpit, if a daughter has had a bad experience in the past, her parents would obviously worry about her future.'

'But they weren't entirely unaware of me, right?'

'Yes, they did know you, and I have told them all about who you are. They know you are a kind person, and they experienced that when you were in Lucknow with us. They have just become a bit skeptical. But don't worry, it's my responsibility to mend it. I will work on that. I'm sorry for all that,' she explained in a way that I couldn't hold onto the hurt for long.

Our communication resumed thereafter, and we spoke on the phone, discussing the trip and our meeting with her parents. By the end of the conversation, we decided to meet in Nagpur.

'Let me give you my undivided attention,' she said. 'We didn't have a good time in Delhi or Lucknow. I know you want to see who I am as a partner, and I wish to understand the same about you. Let's spend a few days together and get to know each other better.'

Despite what happened at her home and her past, Vinee wanted to give it another try, looking beyond horoscopes. While I had reservations about the Lucknow episode, I decided to meet her because I found her to be a nice person and someone I could easily get along with. I also wanted to give this relationship a chance.

'Let's do this,' I agreed.

Nagpur was approximately 120 kilometres away from where she worked in Madhya Pradesh, and near to my work trips as well.

It was a few days before Diwali.

This time, we planned to stay together for a couple of days. I booked a house on Airbnb and made all the necessary arrangements. Since we would be spending two or three days in Nagpur, I decided to book a self-driven car from Zoom Cars upon reaching Nagpur. I drove 120 kilometres to her place to pick her up.

When we were at Futala Lake close to the evening, Vinee shared her past experiences. When she was studying in Delhi, she faced a situation where a guy tried to molest her for a couple of months. She couldn't share it with anyone because she was new in Delhi and was very young at the time, not knowing many people she could ask for help. Eventually, she changed her place of residence to a better PG, and things started to normalise. However, the experience left her with a lingering fear.

I couldn't look her in the eyes as she spoke. My ears were attentive, but my eyes were fixed on the lake, which was surrounded on three sides by forest and a landscaped beach on the fourth side.

'I just couldn't fight him. I wish I could have. I wish I was the woman I am now. He kept on touching me here and there, and all I could do was run away and cry in a corner,' she said.

The sun was setting, and in the evenings, the site was illuminated with halogen lights and Tanga rides (carriage rides). The area was beautiful, with coloured fountains around, but I felt none of that beauty within me. I was consumed with anger, knowing what she suffered and how.

'I think we have seen enough of Nagpur today. Let's head back to the room and continue tomorrow,' I said.

'Sitabuldi Fort is still left. It's just 3 minutes from here. Take a right, Arpit,' she said.

'Where? What?'

'You missed the turn. Now take a U-Turn and then take a left.'

'Look at the time, it must be closed now.'

'It's open 24/7, Google says.'

And then Google Maps announced: Take a left in 200 meters. A minute of a ride, and it announced again: Your destination is on the right.

But when we stepped out of the car and asked the locals, they informed us that the fort is open to the public only three days a year.

I looked at Vinee, shaking my head and smiling. She laughed out loud and said, 'Back to the room it is.'

On our way, she mentioned an incident in Lucknow where she used to live in an isolated area with frequent power outages, making it pitch-dark most of the time.

'One night, while I was riding my scooter, two guys on motorcycles started following me. It was a terrifying experience. They followed me until the end. I knew if I stopped, I would be in trouble. There was no network either, or else I would have called home,' she said. I listened to her without interrupting. She continued, 'They made vulgar comments. I don't know if they were drunk. I could never know. I just raced my scooter and managed to return home safely. Yet, the fear from that incident stayed with me forever. Perhaps, these are the reasons why my family and I are always worried.'

I realised that these experiences had likely contributed to her apprehension towards men. At that point, I felt a strong desire to help her overcome this fear and show her that not all men were the same. I wanted to be her friend and assist her in moving forward.

What really touched me was Vinee's transparency in sharing her past. It brought us closer, allowing me to forgive and forget the episode in Lucknow. I understood how difficult it must have been for her to open up, but she did so because she felt comfortable with me, and that made me comfortable with her.

She also revealed details about her past relationships, including her college ex-boyfriend who had attempted to force himself on her. She immediately ended the relationship, but the trauma stayed with her. After that incident, she wanted to maintain non-physical relationships and give men a chance, but her trust in relationships was repeatedly shattered.

I asked if there was more to share when we reached our temporary home in Nagpur.

Vinee did have more to say.

She talked about a disastrous relationship with a man from Chennai whom she met while completing her Master's degree there. Their relationship ended when he inappropriately questioned her about her physical relationship with her ex-husband. He even dared to call her sister Roshni and ask her about this, and Vinee decided to break up with him.

I knew about the guy from Singapore. She had shared with me about him on our initial calls. He was someone she met from the matrimonial site before me.

Intrigued, I asked her, 'You never told me what went wrong with that man from Singapore.'

'He earned a good income. More than a crore a year. It all began when my family insisted on horoscope matching.'

'A common thing,' I said, smirking. I, too, had to go through this process. 'And, what was the score?'

'Surprisingly, 34 out of 36 Gunas matched,' she said, winking at me.

My eyes lit up. It was a really good match. I knew I was out of the race when it came to horoscope matching.

'So what went wrong,' I asked with genuine curiosity.

'He didn't believe in all that, I understood and was okay with it. But—'

'But what, Vinee?'

'He didn't stay awake for me during the Teej festival when I had to stay awake the entire night,' Vinee replied.

It was part of the ritual for the husband to support his wife in this tradition by staying awake. Even though they were not married, Vinee had started seeing him as her husband. What bothered her was not receiving the same response from him.

I was somewhat surprised by how these relationships ended over seemingly trivial matters. Still, I reminded myself that I couldn't judge or understand the emotions and experiences Vinee had gone through. What mattered was that she chose to share everything with me, and it made me appreciate her openness and honesty.

We stayed there for three days and had a great time with each other. If there were a score out of 36 here, just like in horoscope matching, we would have scored a perfect 36.

During our time in Nagpur, we had a great experience. We explored the city, visited various places, and had deep conversations that helped us understand each other better. I drove her back to her place in Madhya Pradesh, and then I returned to Mumbai to resume my responsibilities.

When Vinee and I were sure, I invited her and her father to my place in Mumbai to arrange a meeting between our families to discuss marriage. Unfortunately, her mother couldn't travel due to health issues, so I couldn't introduce her to my parents, although I wished to.

Roshni was already in Mumbai. She said she could join us any day.

The meeting was planned for November 25th. I had booked tickets for Vinee and her father, who was in Odisha and planned to travel to Mumbai.

However, a sudden turn of events occurred just a few hours before Vinee's scheduled departure.

She messaged me, 'My mother is unwell. I think it's her heart problem. I need to leave for Lucknow immediately, Arpit. I am so sorry. Let's plan this for some other day. Please cancel my train ticket.'

I was disappointed.

Was the universe repeatedly sending me a sign, and I was ignoring it?

———❖❖———

Chapter 10

Promises in Chaos

———◆◆———

Is she fine?

Should I call her father?

Should I call her?

Should I directly go to Lucknow and help her?

I genuinely cared about Vinee's mother and her well-being. But I also knew that I couldn't do anything even if I wanted to. The previous Lucknow episode was rock solid in my mind. Trying to help would be interfering, and that would surely lead to trouble in our relationship.

I also thought about Vinee, and her strength!

She would manage everything there. If she wanted my help, she would let me know. I should wait for her call and not try to interfere.

I looked at my phone. No call or message.

It's a strange thing about waiting for someone's response – you know that there are notifications to let you know if someone has called or messaged, but still, you end up glancing at your mobile screen repeatedly.

'I want to help her, but how?' I thought.

I recalled that my workplace, a cardiac division company, had developed a device that could diagnose heart problems within 10 minutes. This device has been installed in several hospitals in Lucknow over the past few years.

This is it!

Without explicitly stating my intentions to Vinee, I logged into my company's system, found the nearest hospitals from her home with these devices, and sent their addresses to her. I suggested that she take her mother to the hospital nearest to her house.

Though Vinee took some time to respond, she eventually acknowledged my message and promised to consider my suggestion.

'Thanks, Arpit. I'll see what I can do with this,' she replied.

'What's the situation there? Should I come to Lucknow?' I messaged.

I waited and waited for a response. But there was no reply.

Understanding the gravity of the situation, I decided not to press her for more information. Instead, I prayed and hoped that my assistance would contribute to her mother's recovery or proper medical treatment.

The next day, I messaged Vinee to inquire about her mother's condition, 'Hey Vinee, I hope she is fine now. Please take care of yourself too. You forget to eat food and sleep when stressed. We can take care of our family only when we are fine.'

After hitting the send button, I realised I had missed adding something.

'Waiting for your response! Please let me know if you need my help,' I typed and sent it to her.

But… she did not respond. Concerned, I tried to reach out to her several times, receiving no reply. The first call was ignored, the second call as well, and the third too. As time passed, my worry intensified. I attempted to call her, but she did not answer. I even tried reaching out to her father, but I couldn't connect with him.

Continuing my efforts to contact Vinee through calls and messages, I received no response. The growing silence deeply worried me.

'Arpit,' Vinee called me the next day, her voice reflecting tiredness and lack of sleep. 'I want to tell you something.'

'First, tell me about your mother. How is she?' I immediately inquired about her mother's health, expressing my deep concern.

'Umm … she is fine,' Vinee reassured me that her mother was doing well, somewhat easing my initial worry.

Then she confessed something that left me taken aback.

'Arpit, I said I want to tell you something.'

'What is it?' I asked, sensing trouble.

'I lied to you.'

'Lied? What?'

She revealed that she hadn't gone to Lucknow. Instead, she had stayed at her workplace. She had shared my details, like my photograph, date of birth, and full name, with a friend who was an astrologer. This astrologer had made unsettling claims, suggesting that I was involved in black magic.

'Seriously? And you believed her?' I reacted.

Naturally, I was baffled by her admission, as it contradicted my perception of her as a spiritual and positive individual. I expressed my disbelief, asking if she truly believed in such negative ideas.

She explained that she trusted that astrologer and her words had deeply shaken her, instilling fear, which had caused her to withhold our families from meeting each other. She even mentioned staying with her friend for two days due to her anxiety about black magic.

'That was all, Arpit. I lied because I thought you were into black magic and it will harm my personal life once again,' she said from the other side of the call, straight on the tone.

I had my manager breathing down my neck regarding a project, but nothing was more important at that point than talking to Vinee.

I checked my phone and it had an incoming call on waiting from my manager. I am in trouble from both ends!

'Look, Vinee, I seriously don't know what to say. I thought of you as a smart person. Not even in my dreams would I have thought that you would believe in all these things when told by someone else even after spending so much time with me. And me? Into black magic? I don't even feel like explaining myself here,' I said, frustrated, tired, and broken.

I had been calling her these days to check on her mother, all worried. My family was waiting for her family, and upon cancelling the plan, I had to handle them as well. I had managed it all.

And what do I get in return?

I couldn't dismiss this easily; it seemed like a significant red flag. I thought that perhaps she had acted impulsively under her friend's influence. However, I decided to confront the issue honestly, as there was no way to change her newfound beliefs.

In a heartfelt call, I told her that I couldn't help her overcome these fears, and if she truly believed in these things, it might be best for us not to proceed with the marriage.

'What are you saying, Arpit?' Vinee said, seemingly innocent or trying to be.

'That is true! All I can say is that I am not into black magic. And if you don't trust me and believe in such things, let's just not think about our marriage,' I said.

I had to cut the call and get back to my work. I couldn't lose two things in one day. Vinee was past, but I had to save my job.

We had a day of complete silence. I had no hopes of her call or message, and I wasn't actively checking my phone.

It was done from my side.

Then, on the next day, Vinee called me to apologise for the ordeal she had put me through.

'Just listen to me for once before hanging up the call, Arpit,' she said.

I obliged, remaining silent on the call, listening to what she had to say.

She explained that she had consulted two more astrologers for a second opinion, both of whom confirmed that I had no involvement in black magic and that I was a decent person. Their advice was to proceed with the marriage.

I was both relieved and surprised by this news, as I had not expected such a swift resolution to this issue. She expressed regret for her actions, attributing them to her past traumatic experiences.

'As I told you,' she said, 'I know I did wrong by you. But it was because of my past experiences. It's tough to trust someone. I hope you understand. You have all the attributes that I need in my partner. It's just that I wanted to take precautions. My astrologer-friend's suggestion pushed me to take a step back.'

Vinee promised not to bring up these negative beliefs and suggested that we continue with our plans for our families to meet.

I took my time to think. She was a really nice human being. Given that she had a troubled past, resulting in all this mess, I decided to forgive her.

The next day, I called her and asked, 'Is your father still in Mumbai?'

'Yes, he is!' She said, again showing no sign of emotions.

I felt something off. Whether she was detached completely or was it only the straight tone on call, I was not sure. I ignored and focused on the other half of the glass that was full.

Five days after our initial plan, we finally managed to bring our families together.

On her side, it was Vinee, her father, and her sister. My family included my parents, all my sisters, and their husbands. As our families gathered, it was all warmth and smiles, traditional greetings exchanged over chai and sweets.

The initial chatter revolved around my and Vinee's work, our hobbies, and our shared interests: What does Arpit do? What does Vinee do? What are his hobbies? What are her hobbies? Oh! You went there; it's such a nice place. Yes, we believe in it too; our culture is most important.

My parents went on and on with her father, sharing and knowing things.

My sisters, already familiar with Vinee from video calls, effortlessly included her in their conversations. With a quick house tour and settling into a cozy bedroom, the girls indulged in their own lively discussions, taking Roshni with them.

As the day progressed, conversations deepened, touching upon the values dear to both families and their cultural roots. Stories about our lineages were shared, ensuring that our values and ethics aligned seamlessly.

Vinee's father, with a hopeful glint in his eyes, expressed his wish for a life filled with love, respect, and mutual support for us. Amid laughter and shared stories, both families brainstormed ways to weave together customs and rituals for a wedding that honoured both backgrounds.

By the night's end, a sense of connection beyond the marriage arrangement had blossomed. Rooted in shared values, genuine communication, and the promise of a beautiful future, both families had formed a bond that surpassed the mere union of me and Vinee.

On the next day, we gathered again and had also invited our family priest to decide on the auspicious wedding date. Strangely, Vinee suggested not to bother my sisters and their family every single day. I tried to understand her point and agreed to it. My sisters were a bit upset, but I made them understand that we didn't want them to travel every single day. And, anyway, the wedding was going to be close, and they would have joined us for about a fortnight.

The priest proposed two dates – one which was only six days away, and the other which was 4 months away.

Since Vinee was calling the shots, she insisted not to wait, saying, 'Arpit and I had enough time together to know each other. And we can't wait to stay together for four more months.'

Vinee and I both agreed as we felt there was no reason to wait. Our families were also on board with the quick decision, so we decided to go for it.

On the same evening, Bikky's husband and I had a word on call, where he asked, 'Why are you in so much hurry? Take your time, and fix the April date. You both need the space to think it over. Don't make the haste. It's a big decision to get married, brother. You both need to understand each other a bit more before you do.'

I talked to Vinee about it, and we had a good discussion where we concluded that we already know a lot of things about each other, and there is nothing more left.

'I understand your sister's husband's advice, but we have already said yes to the priest and our family. My family is already in preparations, all excited. Why isn't your family on the same page?' Vinee said.

'It's just a perspective,' I said.

'Don't you trust me enough, Arpit?'

'I do! Of course, I do. Anyway, let's not think much, and let's just go for it. We anyway have less time for preparations.'

Our wedding preparations were swift but exciting. We began looking for venues suitable for a gathering of 30-50 people.

'It's only 6 days, how will we manage,' Bikky said.

'Together, we can do anything,' Manisha Didi assured.

We had divided who would do what. My sisters took up the role of decorations and looking after all the important rituals during the wedding week.

'If only we had 100 plus people in each ritual, this would have been a hectic task,' Manisha Didi said. 'Due to lockdown, I know only a few would arrive.'

Finding the venues and booking them was my task. I had shortlisted five places nearby, and needed to see Vinee's perspective. We first had a clear discussion about Mumbai and Lucknow but settled for Mumbai as the wedding place. Since we were booking a near-to-date slot, I personally had to visit the venues and talk to the managers regarding availability and COVID safety. During our search, I noticed Vinee's keen interest and at times a somewhat dominating approach, which was both endearing and a bit irritating.

There was one incident where she seemed to assert herself, criticising, saying, 'Arpit, you are not even capable of finding a good venue. You don't even know what all details one needs to finalise a venue. Men of your age can do such small tasks so easily. You are good at nothing. Why am I even marrying you?'

I really felt bad for what and how she said. I had been expecting her to apologise, which she didn't. Yet, I forgave her thinking that since she is short-tempered, it must have come out of her mouth.

I understood that she basically had specific preferences for the stage, the hall, and even the colour of flowers, among other details. It felt like she was trying to assert herself, but I decided not to argue, thinking that she might be nervous. I preferred that she contribute positively to the planning, rather than just pointing out what not to do.

Given the circumstances, we opted for a small wedding due to the COVID-19 lockdown restrictions. We invited only our closest family members and friends, including my sisters, their families, two of my friends, and two of my father's friends. We did not make elaborate arrangements, as we did not want a big, extravagant wedding. We sent formal invitations to our close ones, but we opted for digital invitations for those who lived far away since we had limited time to coordinate in-person invitations.

The wedding was an intimate affair, with just 28 to 30 people in attendance. It was a bit surprising that none of her relatives could attend the wedding. I had expected some of their immediate family members to be present, but, in the end, only Vinee, her younger sister, and her parents were able to join us.

It was unexpected and surprising!

We initially agreed to split the contribution equally. Vinee, supporting her family, was the main provider as her father neared retirement, and her sister faced challenges in Mumbai. On my side, being the only son, I was the main provider since my dad had retired. However, on the eve of our wedding, Vinee mentioned that only four of her family members could attend, while many from my side would be present. She felt it was unfair for her to contribute half of the wedding expenses. Wanting to maintain the wedding plans and not disappoint her, despite limited savings, I opted to take a loan—my first-ever, which went up to three lakhs and fifty thousand as the expenses grew.

Nonetheless, despite the limited attendance and an urgent loan, we had a wonderful wedding ceremony.

I looked at Vinee during the Saat-Phere, smiled, and thought, 'I hope this works!'

———◆◆———

Chapter 11

Choosing to Forgive, Struggling to Forget

Was I overlooking warning signs? Was I silencing my inner thoughts?

Why?

All to ensure her happiness and the success of our relationship?

Would it truly make a difference? What if it does not?

Could it harm me?

These questions were running in my mind, yet my focus remained on saving the relationship. I wanted to give it a try and make things work.

On our wedding night, she expressed, 'Arpit, I chose you after turning down many.'

I playfully responded, 'Oh! And I thought I was not worth much. By the way, how many rejections are we talking about?'

She casually replied, 'I did not count, but it must be in three digits.'

What?

Curious, I asked, 'Why me?'

Her answer revealed she valued my politeness and humility, qualities she sought in a partner.

It became clear with time that her definition of "humble" meant someone easily influenced. Though I resisted domination, for her, I was willing to adapt.

It felt like a blend of foolishness and love.

I believed in addressing issues rather than giving up on a relationship. I believe people evolve with time.

If Vinee erred, it was my responsibility to guide her, patiently waiting for her to change. However, I needed to retain my identity in the process. I did not want to lose myself being someone's submissive.

It was about maintaining love and self-respect!

Recognising this, I chose to reconnect with her on a personal level, reminiscent of our alone time in Nagpur. This time, it would be in Goa, our honeymoon destination.

Our plan was to stay the night in Shirdi before heading to Goa. As we reached our Shirdi hotel, preparing to visit the temple, Vinee shared one more story of her past.

While I was perusing the hotel restaurant's menu, Vinee dropped a bombshell, revealing her past experience. Emotionally distraught in her marriage, she met a college colleague in Delhi who happened to be a spiritual counsellor.

'He called me at a coffee shop,' Vinee said, 'I discussed my problems with him, and he suggested me to …'

My eyes, ears, all my senses suddenly awakened. I asked, 'What did he suggest?'

'He … he said, to help with my misery and pain, I have to sleep with him.'

'What?' I was shocked.

The silence that followed her words was so deep that I could hear a piece of me breaking. I could not have imagined this even in my dreams.

As a human, I believed it was entirely wrong for a man to ask a helpless woman to sleep with him, or vice versa.

As a partner, rage boiled within me.

Despite that, I trusted Vinee, understanding who she was. Curious, I casually asked, 'And what did you do?'—not fully prepared for her response.

Sheepishly, she admitted, 'We slept together.'

What?

The revelation shattered me, conflicting with my expectations and feelings as her partner. There was this mix of disgust, anger, and betrayal in me. You always hope for a partner you can be 200% sure of; that is the essence of a partnership. Marriage is a commitment built on trust and reliance, sharing an intimate space where you know each other's every detail of life.

Questioning why she had not disclosed this before marriage, I felt a sense of being deceived. Her apology only intensified my confusion.

'Vinee, I want to know why you did not tell me before marriage,' I asked again.

She replied, 'It never came to my mind before.'

Never came to your mind before?

Was it not that important to you?

Was it that casual for you?

When I pressed for details about the guy, she remained silent, refusing to reveal his identity.

Frustrated, I demanded an answer, but she insisted, 'I can't.'

Unable to say much, I left, needing time to process the unexpected revelation and its impact on my life. I just did not want to give a reaction and spoil things up.

After reflecting on the situation for hours all by myself, I accepted the past and decided not to lose her over it. I communicated my feelings, expressing my fear of the present, not the past. She assured me it was behind her, and I resolved to keep our relationship intact, learning from my first marriage's failure.

'See, Vinee, I understand it is all in the past, and I was not in your life then. I want to see the present. I am hoping to have a great present and future life with you.'

She held my hand and said, 'Me too, Arpit. Me too!'

We moved forward, seeking a fresh start and blessings from Sai Baba in Shirdi. Subconsciously, however, the past lingered within me, connecting the dots from the first conversation to her revelation in Shirdi—multiple red flags I had ignored for the sake of making things work.

On the night of our Shirdi trip, unable to sleep, I looked at her and realised I needed to be cautious in dealing with her. Partners should be reliable, and I acknowledged that my life might become challenging. Despite telling her it was in the past, I felt cheated and had lingering anger.

As a partner, I felt a fit of boiling anger, simultaneously sorry for the person I married. However, I still had deep affection for her the moment I heard her voice, saw her face-to-face, and when she started caring for me. It was a mix of conflicting emotions—good and bad, yet a strong fondness remained.

I thought that if she wanted to keep it hidden, she would not have shared it with me at all. There was no way I would have known this. She was honest and shared without any confrontation, expressing her comfort as my partner.

One part of me hesitated to trust her, while another urged me to try and make it work, to be patient, and to strive for improvement.

I stood up, and walked into the bathroom while she was still sleeping. Turning on the bathroom light, I splashed water on my face, thoughts racing through my mind.

She could have said all this before the wedding also. Why is she telling me now? Does she want to sabotage our relationship? Is it because she knows that now we are married, and nothing worse can happen if she opens up about it?

I learned two traits about her after this episode:

1. Her ability to handle herself in the time of distress.

2. She can be easily manipulated by someone to keep her dignity at stake.

Looking at the mirror, I questioned myself, 'Did I get married to the wrong person?'

Chapter 12

The Silent Burden of Betrayal

By morning, the optimistic side of me prevailed. I decided to give it a try, putting in my effort to help her move past her history. I realised why, in the first instance, I had married her. From whatever she had shared about her, I knew she had a difficult past, and I wanted to give her what she rightfully deserved. Hence, I never wanted to give up but see her happy.

I believed in the philosophy, "If you don't find a better one, try to make the one you found better."

Recognising her troubled past, I was determined that things could change. Making this marriage work became a primary goal in my life, prioritising it above all else.

Reflecting on the previous night, I realised our upcoming honeymoon trip could have been disastrous. However, when the positive side in me prevailed, it turned into one of the most memorable experiences of our lives. We returned to Mumbai from Nashik on a 5-hour road trip and headed to Goa the next day.

Our journey to and from Goa was by flight, a gift from me, covering all expenses for the 6-day trip. I arranged a car for internal travel and ensured we stayed in a comfortable 3-star hotel without compromising on food. My aim was to create every opportunity for her to forget her past and make her fall in love with me.

We engaged in adventurous activities like banana rides, paragliding, jet-skiing, scuba diving, and more. Despite her fear of water, I encouraged her to try water sports. There was a moment when she had tequila shots and was drunk to the brim.

I asked her, 'Let's dance?'

'You and dance?' Vinee reacted.

'Yes! I like to dance,' I said.

'You sisterf*cker, you didn't tell me this before the wedding,' she said, high on alcohol, not realising her language.

'Vinee! That is too much. Watch your language.'

'Chill dude! Why are you getting offended? I anyway didn't abuse your sister.'

I hate abusive language, but just because she was drunk, I let her have that benefit of the doubt.

I drove her back to the hotel, making sure not to drink so that I could safely handle the situation and avoid any trouble.

Our time in Goa was delightful, and I was eager to build new memories for us, striving for a happy life ahead. We enjoyed a romantic dinner on a cruise one evening, creating some beautiful moments.

'The cruise under the starlit sky is truly magical, Arpit. Thanks for suggesting this romantic dinner,' she said, her eyes all around.

'I'm glad you liked the idea, Vinee. The ocean breeze and the sound of the waves make it even more special, right?'

'It does. And the way the moonlight reflects on the water, it is like nature itself is celebrating our love.'

I gave a smile, saying, 'I could not agree more. It feels like a scene from a movie.'

'Likewise, Arpit. Here's to us and our beautiful moments,' she said, raising her glass to toast.

'To us,' I said raising my glass of wine.

We clinked glasses, enjoying the cruise and savouring the beautiful moments we were creating together. However, despite the good times, the lingering bad thoughts persisted.

Though not a professional photographer, I attempted to capture her photos, exploring various angles, but she did not like any of them.

Despite my efforts, she continued to criticise, repeating, 'You don't know this! You don't know that!'

Feeling upset one night, I went as far as searching on YouTube to learn how to take better photographs just for her. Unfortunately, my sincere efforts were not appreciated; instead, I received a lot more of criticism from her. She expressed her dissatisfaction, stating, 'You have clicked like an idiot. I too will turn an idiot if I stay with you.'

Despite constant criticism for every small thing, making me feel inadequate, I was determined not to give up on her. Just a week after marriage, instead of contemplating separation, I remained positive, focusing on finding ways to make things better.

After spending two days with us in Mumbai, she had to return to her place in Madhya Pradesh for her job. I made regular visits whenever I could. Knowing she couldn't relocate to Mumbai soon, I requested my office to find a way for me to work from her city.

While my boss said they were looking into it, I realised the chances of securing a job in her city were slim. Despite the uncertainty, we promised each other to meet and spend weekends together. Whether she traveled to Mumbai or I visited her in Madhya Pradesh, our plan was to figure out how to stay together permanently in less than six months.

My first trip to her city, where I stayed with her for two days, had both positive and negative moments. During dinner on a Saturday night, I inquired about her week at the office.

She shared, 'It was great rejoining. My colleagues wished me, and we had my wedding party on Thursday, as I told you. But, you know, this interlibrary loan thing really frustrated me.'

Curious, I asked, 'What is this loan?'

She expressed surprise, exclaiming, 'Interlibrary loan. It is... wait! How come you don't know? Everyone knows!'

I defended, 'There might be people who don't, right?'

Her response was cutting, 'Such people are grown-up fools.'

Challenged, I questioned, 'Are you saying I am a fool?'

She bluntly stated, 'Yes, you are. It's such an easy thing. See, I told you. You are good for nothing. You don't even have common knowledge about things.'

Feeling disheartened that night, I decided to look up what "Interlibrary loan" meant online. I discovered that it is a service offered by libraries to borrow materials from another library on behalf of a patron, expanding access to a wider range of resources. Librarians manage this process, coordinating borrowing and lending between different libraries.

I realised I knew the concept, I just didn't know what it was called. Despite this, I felt that as a partner, she shouldn't have demoralised me. If our roles were reversed, I would have gently explained what it meant. The criticism left me feeling disheartened once again.

The friction in our relationship surfaced even before marriage, it came to light more clearly after it and became apparent in February 2021. With her birthday on the 4th and our first Valentine's Day approaching on the 14th, I decided to plan something special to fix the gap between us.

Excitedly, she joined in as we explored various destinations in India, particularly focusing on places in the South and West for an outing in the jungle or a Jungle Safari—an experience we both desired.

Gir Forest in Gujarat seemed perfect, but it was too far for us and wouldn't allow for extended leave from our offices. Considering our limitations, we searched for nearby options and settled on Pench National Park, just one to two hours from Nagpur, aligning well with our plans.

Handling operations for our company in Maharashtra allowed me to manage a few tasks even during our trip.

Keen to surprise her, I deviated from our initial plan of arriving on the 4th, her birthday, and instead, I arrived on the 3rd. Since IRCTC limits users to six bookings per month, and my travel frequency had already exhausted that quota, I booked a ticket from her father's account, registered on my phone, for a journey from Mumbai to her city in Madhya Pradesh. However, this led to her father receiving a notification, prompting him to inform his daughter of my early arrival.

She called me, saying, 'You are coming, and you didn't even tell me.'

I explained, 'It was supposed to be a surprise.'

She was somewhat happy to discover the surprise I had planned for her. I had arranged balloons, cake, teddy bears, and flowers. Even the landlords of her rented apartment joined the celebration. I hosted a dinner party and invited them and their children.

While the landlord and his family opted for their car, Vinee and I were on her scooter. The cold was intense, and we were shivering. Throughout the ride, she complained about the cold and how it would make her sick. On the way back home, I suggested driving slowly to avoid catching a cold, or she could ride with the landlord in the car. Without a moment's hesitation, she chose to go back in the car, not even glancing back at me.

As a partner, I expected that we would face any weather together, be it cold or hot.

I was expecting her to say something like, "It is okay. I will hug you from the back."

I found myself alone, riding back on the scooter in the cold, while she chose the comfort of the car.

I tried to reassure myself, saying, 'It is okay, Arpit. Things will be good soon.'

On the 13th, we were on our three-day trip to Pench National Park. I had rented a car from Zoom Cars, and our journey from Nagpur to Pench was full of anticipation. We had booked a luxurious five-star hotel nestled inside the jungle, surrounded by lush greenery, creating a truly beautiful setting.

Upon checking into our room, the excitement reached a different level as we revelled in luxury and comfort.

On the first night, in our private space, I asked her, 'How do you feel here?'

She unintentionally responded, 'It is so nice here, Rohit...'

Rohit was the name of her ex-boyfriend from Chennai. Realising the mistake, she fell silent. She understood that she had mentioned Rohit's name instead of mine. I was shocked and felt that she might still be in contact with him, leaving me broken and upset.

Immediately, I said, 'I want to see your phone.'

She assertively responded, 'No.'

Flashbacks flooded my mind, stirring anger, frustration, irritation, and perplexity. Whatever happened in her life before our relationship didn't bother me, but being her partner, her husband, if she was still in touch with someone else, that was a complete turn-off for me.

I did not say a word when she criticised me. I did not say a word when she put me down. I did not say a word when she said I'm good for nothing.

I had avoided confrontation for the sake of making our relationship work.

However, this was not acceptable!

I snatched her phone and started scrolling through the chats. I came across a conversation with someone other than Rohit – a person named Pawan from Delhi. I recalled she had mentioned this friend who was experiencing difficulties in his marriage, a married man with a child.

A few days earlier, Vinee had posted a video of herself doing yoga. Pawan had sent her a message, stating that she looked hot. This exchange of private messages occurred after our wedding.

I continued scrolling down.

On January 26th, there was an important event at her Kendriya Vidyalaya. As it is a central government school, days like January 26, August 15, and October 2 are important, and all staff members are required to be present. On such occasions, women are expected to wear sarees, and Vinee had worn one as well.

As I continued scrolling through the chats, I discovered that she had sent a picture of herself in a saree to Pawan. He replied, stating that she looked gorgeous.

In one chat, Vinee had told Pawan, "No! I can never break his trust."

However, she had deleted the message where he asked her to do something that she refused, citing she couldn't break my trust. I was perplexed about what he had asked her to do, and it triggered me.

Such exchanges with anyone after getting married felt inappropriate to me. Moreover, she hadn't disclosed anything about it, not even that she was talking to someone. Thirdly, she was not revealing the complete truth, and this constant concealment intensified my hurt.

We argued about this for days, yet she never disclosed the content of the message. The fact that she was consistently hiding it added to my pain and raised numerous questions in my mind. I couldn't focus on anything else.

I reached a point where I told myself, 'Even if she tells me the truth and expresses remorse, I swear I would forgive her.'

However, she never did. She showed no remorse.

I cried in front of her, pleading, 'You told me about your Delhi friend asking you to sleep with him. You were open about it in Shirdi. Why not now? Please tell the truth. Help me save this relationship.'

But she remained unyielding, arguing and avoiding any confession.

This wasn't the end of something but the beginning of the worst.

——◆◆——

Chapter 13

Is Narcissism Raining?

From that day on, our relationship became a constant cycle of ups and downs. I made efforts to solve things, but my attempts fell short. Frustrated, I would drop the topic, giving her yet another chance.

The persistent feeling of demotivation in our interactions was deeply painful. She would frequently tell me, 'You are not even good at managing your job.'

All of these experiences transformed me into someone unrecognisable. Confidence waned, hope diminished, and goals seemed distant. I questioned who I was compared to my earlier self.

The right partner can uplift and transform, but the wrong one has the power to destroy.

I began to internalise her criticisms, thinking that if my own partner viewed me this way, then perhaps I was the problem. Self-criticism took over, and unknowingly, I slipped into depression.

I always aimed to be the hero in her eyes, doing everything within my capacity. Little did I realise that I wasn't lacking; she was at fault for not making effort. It was only later that I recognised I was married to a narcissist, discovering the term through reading books and online resources.

A narcissist is an individual characterised by excessive self-love, a heightened sense of their own importance, and a lack of empathy for others. Narcissists often seek admiration and validation from others, exaggerate their achievements, and display a sense of entitlement. They may exploit relationships for personal gain and struggle to recognise or care about the needs and feelings of others.

In their behaviour, narcissists can be manipulative, controlling, and prone to outbursts when their self-image is threatened. They may engage in grandiose fantasies and have difficulty accepting criticism. Despite appearing confident, their self-esteem is often fragile, leading to a constant pursuit of validation. Relationships with narcissists can be challenging, as their focus on themselves can overshadow the needs and well-being of those around them.

Everything I read about narcissism seemed to align with her nature. Because of her, I distanced myself from friends, not meeting them for months, and even had conflicts with my family. When she visited Mumbai briefly, I was solely focused on being with her, neglecting any interaction with my family. My mother, sensing the signs, tried to warn me, but I dismissed her concerns, believing Vinee to be a nice person who needed time.

My mother accepted that my life was going to be difficult, realising Vinee's true nature. Despite her trying to be a mother figure, Vinee didn't reciprocate.

I pretended to be busy when I was free, hoping for her acknowledgment. I craved her compliments, always striving for her respect, but she never offered it.

I came to realise that her main goal was domination, and unfortunately, I played the role of the fool who allowed it.

In late March, feeling broken and sad, I decided to spend time alone to figure out what to do. I booked a resort in Uttan and stayed there for a day, deliberately not answering her calls or messages. I needed to detach to understand what I could do with my life. My personal issues were affecting my professional life, and the efforts I had put into yoga and meditation were nullified. I needed time alone to reflect.

Amidst contemplation, I turned to drinking, questioning myself about where I was in life and what I was doing.

"Stop spoiling your life," I almost yelled at myself.

Having consumed four bottles of beer, I was deep in darkness, ignoring her calls and messages. Feeling lost about my life, I reached out to my school friends. Unaware of the turmoil in my personal life, they believed I was happily married and focused on my new life. When I finally opened up to them, they were shocked.

One friend rushed to pick me up, and we headed to Bandra to meet the others. They patiently listened as I poured out my struggles. Their conclusion was clear – I needed to talk to Vinee and express everything I felt about our relationship.

'Whatever frustration, anger, or self-doubt you are carrying, share it with her. She deserves to know,' Aman advised.

'If she understands, great. If not, you know what to do. We can't see you like this,' Karan added.

'You were never like this before. Get everything out and tell her. We want our old Arpit back,' Aman highlighted.

They advised me that holding things in would lead to more depression, making everything tougher. As I had been drinking continuously since the afternoon, my friends dropped me home. The evening left me tense, unable to sleep as I pondered over their suggestions.

I promptly booked an early morning flight from Mumbai to Nagpur.

I hadn't slept properly, my eyes were swollen, appearing weak. I somehow reached Nagpur, but lacking a train reservation, I took a bus from Nagpur to her place in Madhya Pradesh. It was the most difficult journey of my life, but reaching her was necessary.

Vinee was not expecting me; she was surprised.

'What are you doing here?' She reacted, not a sign of happiness in her tone.

'Should I come inside first?' I said, straight to my mission.

As the door closed, I started letting out whatever was in my heart and mind. I had told myself not to do something stupid, not to get violent or throw things around, which I never was. I did what I could with my voice. I spoke and spoke, letting it out.

'… and you think I am good for nothing,' I said, losing my voice, crying, anger and frustration in my tone.

Instead of comforting me, she grabbed her phone and threw it on the ground, breaking it into pieces, and ran inside the kitchen. I followed her in to see she wouldn't harm herself. It was strange how I cared for her even at that point in time when I was the one who needed comfort. So many things happened, and I was broken so much, that I was surprised by how things turned out. I came outside the kitchen right away. She didn't follow me out, shouting and crying from the kitchen, while I sat on the sofa, my hands on my face. I knew I had to maintain the space before anything worse happened.

"You are here to talk," I reminded myself. "Only talk."

When she stopped screaming, I went back to the kitchen and asked her, 'Do you want to talk in peace for us?'

She didn't answer.

I asked again and again. But she didn't reply.

I called her father and told him everything. She was screaming in the background while I was sharing about Vinee's chats with her father. I told him what she said about my family. She said shitty things about my mother and sisters. My sister told her that she has some clothes that won't fit her because she has gained weight but it will be of good use to Vinee. But when I told Vinee about it, her response shocked me. I was angry and hurt about what she said about my mother and sisters. It kind of made me sad and depressed.

'How can she say it? It is actually good that we are not staying with my parents or else, this must have been much worse. Please help her understand,' I concluded talking to my father-in-law.

I cried while talking to him. I felt weak emotionally, physically, and mentally. Vinee looked at me without showing any concern. Normally, one would feel bad if someone close is broken and crying in front of you, but she didn't seem to care. She didn't try to comfort me, hug me, or help me stop crying. Instead, she took out her iPhone and acted busy with it, giving a very cold response.

I went searching for answers at her place but came back to Mumbai with more questions on my mind.

Never push someone to the point where they lose all fear.

I became that person.

I was changing, but not for the better. I reached a point where I questioned who I had become, realising that I was losing my character and identity since we got married.

Dark thoughts started to invade my mind.

I stayed with her at the Madhya Pradesh's residence for weeks during the lockdown, working from home.

I initially came to express my feelings, crying and letting out my emotions. I realised that for things to improve between us, staying together was crucial. Despite the tension, I chose to settle with her, knowing that being apart would never resolve anything.

We avoided talking to prevent fights, but I believed that staying together offered a chance for us to mend our relationship.

I never considered ending our relationship even for a moment. Despite facing numerous challenges, I always hoped we could overcome them. I put in significant effort to make our relationship work, and I was determined to continue until the very end. Despite being broken, crying, and enduring confusion, I never entertained the thought of giving up. When I went to her place that day, it was to express my feelings and share the troubles in my heart, not to end things between Vinee and me.

I personally believe that if you have not given your best and unlocked your full potential to salvage a relationship, you should not give up.

Nowadays, people lack patience, and even a minor issue leads to separation. If everyone follows this pattern, relationships will constantly break. It is important to give your best to save a relationship.

While decisions may be necessary when things escalate, why decide when only a single drop is in?

Marriage should not be given up easily.

In today's practical world, having faith and patience in important relationships is essential.

In my persistent efforts, I discovered another reason for us to stay together.

In April, Vinee's pregnancy news emerged during the intense second wave and strict lockdown.

As her third month approached with a missed period, we initially attributed it to irregular dates. However, when it happened for the third time, I suggested a pregnancy test, and the results confirmed she was pregnant.

'Are you serious?' I asked her.

She showed me the test result, and it brought an immediate smile to my face. Despite our strained relationship and lack of communication, the news made me very happy.

When she asked about continuing the pregnancy or considering abortion, I interrupted, saying, 'That is not the question. I am genuinely happy. I want this baby, Vinee. Hopefully, it could bring us together again.'

I began searching for the best gynaecologist in the city. Using an ultrasound test, we needed to assess the foetus's size and inquire about necessary precautions. We aimed for the best care, and we needed it promptly.

I located a good gynaecologist 30 kilometres away from our location, and we booked a private cab to get there. After the checkup, we learned that she was already three months pregnant.

We immediately informed our respective families, and they were thrilled with the news. Both families and Vinee and I were happy. I saw this as a potential turning point in our relationship, believing that our bond would improve from here on. I felt very hopeful and happy.

I attempted a heart-to-heart conversation with her during a walk on our terrace.

I said, 'Now that something beautiful is ahead of us, we need to have an accepting mindset. There will be times when we won't like each other's actions, but we must find better ways to communicate. Can we agree on that?'

She replied, 'I don't say anything wrong. It is always you messing things up. So, I think this is applicable to you.'

Though I hoped for a ceasefire, I accepted the situation and focused on what I could control—myself. I devised a strategy: fewer conversations to minimise friction. I decided to limit communication during that period to avoid stressing her during her pregnancy, making it my primary plan to move forward.

I aimed for her to have a stress-free pregnancy and was willing to do anything for it. I inquired about her preferred location during pregnancy – whether Lucknow, her hometown, or Mumbai, my hometown. I preferred Mumbai for two reasons. First, my family's presence, and second, Mumbai offered excellent medical facilities with good hospitals. In contrast, Lucknow, where she lived, was distant from the main city. Medical facilities, especially a good gynaecologist, were not easily accessible, requiring a 20 to 30-kilometre travel, something I wanted to avoid for her.

'From that perspective, it would be better if we go to Mumbai and get the baby delivered there,' I requested.

She instantly denied, having persistent issues with my family members, always interpreting positive steps negatively.

She decided on Lucknow, stating, 'I will get my delivery done in Lucknow only. I won't go to Mumbai in any case.'

I respected her decision—I had to—prioritising her comfort.

Fortunately, due to the pregnancy, we began having normal conversations. Until August, I took care of her, doing my best as a husband. I arranged private taxis for appointments with a gynaecologist in Nagpur, a four-hour journey. I had chosen this doctor from the city, aware that there were no qualified gynaecologists in that city, and I wanted the best care for Vinee and our child. Nagpur was not too far, so I selected that doctor as our guide from April to July.

In July, on my birthday, Vinee planned a surprise at a place called Cafechino. She arranged a cake and more surprises.

Things were getting normal between us; the spark of love was reigniting. She took steps to mend the issues between us. And that was the best feeling I ever hoped for.

My life was back to normal.

But then, I received a call from my sister, saying, 'Arpit, Papa has collapsed. We are taking him to a hospital.'

Chapter 14

Strong, Patient, but Broken

My sister informed me that my father had collapsed, and his blood pressure was dropping. Fortunately, I worked for a company with a team of doctors who could quickly assess heart problems within 5-10 minutes. The ECG machine from my office happened to be in my Mumbai house.

'Get on a video call,' I told my sister.

I guided her on how to connect the ECG machine with the phone and how to connect the lead cables to Papa's chest, hands, and legs, and she performed the test on our father. The results were critical, indicating a problem with his heart. My sisters immediately rushed him to the nearest hospital on the same day.

When a family member is suffering, and you're far away, regret sets in. However, you do everything within your capacity to make things right. Though I felt bad about not being there, I made sure I stayed updated by having my sisters inform me regularly.

Our father had a checkup and angiography the next day, revealing multiple blocked arteries. Doctors warned of a potential massive heart attack at any moment.

Upon hearing the news, I traveled from Nagpur to Mumbai via flight. I met with the doctor who conducted the angiography, and he recommended bypass surgery.

It was a shocking news for us.

'You really need to ask someone,' I told myself.

I consulted the CEO of my company, also a cardiologist in Bangalore. After emailing him the reports, he strongly recommended immediate bypass surgery.

'Don't waste time, Arpit,' he instructed on call.

Despite the tension in my family, we made the decision and went through with the surgery. It was a painful journey for my father, who spent 13 days in the hospital post-surgery. After discharge, we took care of him, providing a walker for mobility. We hired a caretaker to assist with his daily needs.

Once I felt the situation was stable, I returned to my wife's place in Madhya Pradesh. Balancing my father's health with my wife's pregnancy became the biggest responsibility. I had to go up and down to take care of both.

Vinee was glad to see me back. It was really good how she regularly called to check on my father when I was in Mumbai. Surprisingly, when I was about to leave for Mumbai, she suggested accompanying me. However, given the tense situation in my family, I advised her, 'Please stay peacefully here.'

I did not want her to see the suffering.

In Mumbai, we struggled to have proper meals as everyone was focused on my father's surgery. Fortunately, in our home in Madhya Pradesh, a maid cooked and took care of Vinee. I didn't want to compromise on her health even a bit.

In the later stage of pregnancy, I took her to Lucknow, ensuring all details were sorted – the doctor, location, travel time, expenses, and emergency plans. I had a clear plan of what to do and what not to do.

Everything progressed well. Vinee and our child were healthy, thanks to early precautions. Her family was actively involved in preparations too. The hospital in Lucknow was about 20 kilometres from her place, so we sought counselling from the lady doctor, examined all the facilities, and met the assistant doctors. I explored other hospitals but stuck with the same one since the doctor and facilities were satisfactory.

The 7-8 days I spent with her in Lucknow were really good; everything was normal between us. I had a great time with her parents as well, and I left only after I saw everything was perfect.

I returned to Mumbai and resumed taking care of my father. During my absence, one of my sisters handled duties, but I took control upon my return, managing his hospital visits.

The surgery incurred significant expenses, and I had to invest my time in both Mumbai and Lucknow for two most important people in my life. I felt drained emotionally, physically, and financially.

I understood that I had no support but it was okay and manageable until something unexpected happened.

Just a month after the surgery, I received a call from Vinee, requesting ₹50,000.

'I took a loan from my friend before our marriage, and I need to give him back. Please, it's urgent,' she said.

'I really have to manage, Vinee. Give me some time. I will arrange the money. But, Vinee, who is this friend you are talking about?' I asked.

Abruptly and arrogantly, she replied, 'Don't ask me so many questions. Give the money if you can or just leave it.'

'You don't have to be so rude. You know my situation. You know what we are going through. You know how much money has been spent in the last couple of months. My father has just come out of bypass surgery and about the monthly expenses after the surgery. You know everything about this.'

'Don't give me the lecture. Just say no if you can't,' she said and cut the call without letting me speak.

I was disappointed.

Amidst all these loads and tension, our regrowing bond was my mental anchor. However, her recent behaviour pushed me back to square one.

Throughout the month, she taunted me on various topics.

During one such call, she said, 'You haven't even added me to your salary account. I don't even know what your salary is.'

'I have shown you my salary slip. Why bring this up now when my father is unwell and you're pregnant? Why stress about it?' I replied.

'But I am not added to your salary account.'

'What difference does that make? Only if you're added, you will trust me?'

I couldn't believe that she was showing very little concern for my mental well-being. Why couldn't she understand my financial situation? Why wasn't she being sensitive?

I started thinking if she had married me only for my money. Was it only because I was the only son of my parents and that my parents were too old?

Despite these thoughts, I convinced myself to focus on the positives, reminding myself of the upcoming beautiful addition to our lives – the baby we were supposed to have.

I chose not to create unnecessary conflict and told myself, 'Focus on positives rather than negatives.'

After that incident, I had to go to Bangalore for my quarterly meeting, and I really wanted to calm things between us. Hence, I sent flowers and a greeting card from Ferns N Petals.

I was born this way, a very positive person. I initiated conversations with her, aiming to lighten the mood. However, there was an instance when she shouted at me in her mother's presence.

In a lifelong relationship, it's important to share complaints directly with your partner rather than making a public display of them. Respecting your partner is one of the core, and Vinee seemed to be doing the opposite.

I tried to address it, saying, 'Vinee, please don't do that. Your family would panic for no reason. Just don't.'

Despite my request, she wouldn't listen and escalated the situation into a huge fight.

I had already booked my tickets to Lucknow. To prevent further disputes, I realised meeting her in person was necessary. I also wanted to be with her during her pregnancy while managing my father's health in Mumbai.

'I can't have such a scenario between us, especially when she is weeks away from delivery,' I reminded myself.

Despite her repeated insistence on adding her to my salary account, Vinee and I had always ended up fighting over this topic on calls.

Just a day before my flight, I got to know about the accident.

Vinee's parents were on a motorcycle when a speeding car collided with them from behind. It wasn't their fault; they were riding on one side of the road, unaware of what awaited them.

Vinee's father was thrown off the road with a jolt, his chest pounding on the pavement, the audible sound of his ribcage breaking. He suffered multiple fractures internally. However, it was her mother who faced a deadly accident. Her face collided with the car and it literally drove over her face, dragging her for almost 50 meters.

The car's driver noticed her mistake and stopped. She was unaware of the lady being dragged with the car, but by then, a lot of damage had been done. One side of her face skin was torn, with flesh and blood everywhere. She suffered a degloving injury, where the top layer of her face skin and tissue tore away. Additionally, she had a severe injury to her right leg, damaging the muscle and bone.

I saw the photos that Vinee had sent me and was shattered. I couldn't stop crying.

Despite being the cause of the accident, the lady took them to a government hospital with the help of people nearby. While there is no justification for her actions, the fact that she didn't flee and brought them to the hospital immediately helped save two lives. However, the damage, especially to Vinee's mother, was severe, and she was critically ill with a high chance of passing away.

As soon as her father could communicate, he contacted Vinee from inside the car and informed her about the accident. Vinee, crying and wailing, immediately called me and shared everything.

Normally composed, I lost my calm upon hearing the news. I began to panic and cry loudly. My parents, sensing the severity of my reactions on the call, tried to calm me down. This was also because of the back-to-back incidents that were happening. It was that stage of my life where I completely lost control over myself and my emotions, with so much happening around me. There were so many things going on inside me, feelings that were suppressed and were let out that day. All of the incidents, and the frictions between Vinee and me, were stored up. I didn't react to it for months, but now, it was all coming out.

I sat there, staring into the unknown, watching my tears roll down my face and I then realised I was under so much stress. It seemed like the floodgates had burst open and all the pent-up feelings rushed out of me. The conflicts with Vinee, the pressure due to recent occurrences, and personal issues and anxieties were overwhelming. I could hear my parents fretting and their efforts to console me made me cry even more. I have to admit that, in that moment, I knew that I could not take it anymore. It was time for me to stand up to these emotions and look for the ways to cope with everything in my life.

'Arpit, this is not the time for you to lose it. You are not only our only son but also theirs,' my mother said. 'They need you. You have to be strong. Vinee needs you, especially during her pregnancy.'

'Arpit, son, you need to go there immediately,' my father suggested, and I heeded his advice.

Given the ongoing COVID period with no common direct flights, I decided to figure out the best route to reach there. Instead of waiting for the next day's scheduled flight, I rushed to the airport to catch the earliest available flight. My priority was to be beside Vinee as soon as possible.

On my way, I called my immediate boss and tearfully explained the situation. My emotional state surprised him.

'Just calm down, Arpit,' he advised. 'I understand it is a tough situation, but I have never seen you so lost. If you're going now, be strong to take care of them. If you can't be strong, consider taking a day or two before leaving. You won't be of help if you're in need yourself.'

I shared the photos Vinee sent me and explained the situation about my in-laws. I was shaken and confused, which I am usually not, be it any situation.

After the call ended, I searched for the next flight while traveling in an autorickshaw from Bhayander to Vile Parle. Realising there were no direct or indirect flights to Lucknow until the next morning, and taking a train would be impractical, I decided to wait. It was around 9 at night, and I had a few hours before the morning flight. I instructed the driver to turn back home.

I couldn't sleep the entire night, the distance weighing heavily on me. We were in the hall when my father suggested taking my mother with me.

'Yes, let me come with you,' my mother said. 'Vinee and her parents need me too. We can together look after them. Also, Vinee needs homemade food during pregnancy. She should not take so much load. I will manage the house, and you can focus on the hospital.'

'Vinee shouldn't be troubled with hospital visits. She herself needs attention. Take your mother along,' my father added.

Concerned, I asked, 'What about you, Papa? Who will look after you?'

'Soni and Sweety are both coming tomorrow morning. I'll ask one of them to stay here for a few days. Don't worry about me. You go and take care of the father and mother who need you,' he assured.

I informed Vinee on the call that my mother and I were coming in the morning. She responded, 'My sister is in Mumbai too. Please bring her along. I don't understand, Arpit. Anything can happen with Mumma. At least Roshni should see her one last time if anything happens.'

'Don't say that, please. Nothing will happen to our mother,' I comforted her.

'Hmm,' she sighed. 'What about father? How is he?'

'You'll see tomorrow when you arrive. Please bring Roshni. Bye! I need to go to the hospital. I am alone here anyway,' she said and ended the call.

I couldn't understand her response, but my focus was on my in-laws, especially my mother-in-law. Her health had always been challenging – she was a highly diabetic patient and had suffered a previous paralysis attack. The survival percentage was low. With multiple injuries, her face torn apart, she underwent surgery lasting around 5-6 hours.

Panicking, I mistakenly booked tickets to Varanasi instead of Lucknow, losing almost ₹35,000 due to the high prices and no refund policy. After calming myself, I rebooked three tickets to Lucknow via New Delhi for an early morning flight, reaching in 4-5 hours.

I called Roshni, providing flight details. She, too, was in tears, and I tried to talk to her. Advising her to get some sleep before the busy day, I realised it was easier said than done, as I struggled to sleep that night myself.

I stayed in constant touch with Vinee, taking hourly updates. By then, I called my relatives in Lucknow and they had reached the hospital, providing support to Vinee and her parents throughout the night. They took care of Vinee, shuttling her between the hospital and home.

I suggested my cousin-sister take Vinee for an ultrasound test to check on the baby. Amidst caring for my in-laws and Vinee, it was of utmost importance to have someone monitoring the baby's well-being, especially considering she was eight months pregnant.

'The baby is fine,' my cousin said, and I smiled for the first but only for a minute that week.

We arrived in Lucknow at around 11:30 AM. As soon as Vinee saw me, she ran and hugged me tightly, tears streaming down her face. I held her in my arms, running my fingers through the back of her head to comfort her.

Without delay, we headed to the hospital. My father-in-law seemed better; he could talk and was in his hospital bed. However, my mother-in-law's condition was extremely severe, even worse than the photos suggested. I didn't have the strength to witness it, it was that distressing.

My sole focus was to give my utmost and do everything in my power to support my family. I couldn't bear to see the pain they were enduring. I assumed the role of a devoted son, taking on all responsibilities. Visiting the hospital 4-5 times a day, I stayed there for hours before returning to care for Vinee.

Amidst the stress and care, Vinee never let her guard down, often finding reasons to argue. Three days after the accident, while at home with Vinee and my mother, Roshni called from the hospital.

'Jijaji (Brother-in-law), please don't bring Vinee Di to the hospital,' she requested. I couldn't reply much, as Vinee was sitting beside me, trying to understand the conversation.

Roshni continued, 'Whenever she comes to the hospital, she fights with the nurses, blaming them for not taking care of our mother. She argues with the doctors too, forgetting that these are the same people caring for our mother.'

Vinee, curious, asked, 'What is she saying? Put it on speaker,' coming closer to hear the conversation. I shook my head, signalling that it was not something important.

I replied to Roshni stepping away from Vinee so that she doesn't hear me, 'I think it's because it's a government hospital, and—'

'Exactly, Jijaji,' Roshni cut me off and continued, 'We can't expect private hospital treatment from a government hospital, but they are doing all that is required.'

I whispered to Roshni, 'Maybe it's because Vinee feels our mother should be treated in a particular manner. We can't blame her; she is worried.'

'Even if she feels the doctors and nurses aren't caring the way she wants, there's a proper way to express it. Inappropriately arguing with them is the reason they might not be taking adequate care of our mother,' Roshni conveyed.

Vinee, persistently asking for updates, followed me around the house. Roshni urged me to talk to Vinee immediately.

'Talk to her now, Jijaji. I don't want her to come to the hospital and do this,' Roshni insisted.

Feeling caught in the middle, I suggested Roshni talk directly to Vinee about it. When Roshni agreed, I handed the phone to Vinee, not wanting to be in the crossfire.

The heated conversation between Roshni and Vinee played out audibly. After Vinee disconnected, she started shouting at me.

'I was asking you for so long what she was saying. I told you to keep the phone on speaker. You don't even understand such a thing, you useless man,' Vinee berated me.

Roshni, rightfully or not, had shouted at Vinee during their conversation. It was disheartening how Vinee directed her anger at me without reason.

My mother was present, witnessing everything.

'Beta, why have we come here? To take care of you and the family, right?' my mother tried to intervene.

Vinee didn't respond to my mother but gave her a resentful look.

'Vinee,' I intervened, breaking the intense stare. 'Respect the situation, please. This reaction of yours is not justified. Just calm down!'

However, she didn't stop; the shouting continued. My mother, witnessing Vinee's behaviour, was very much surprised. When my mother tried to speak up, she blacked out due to high blood pressure. She had this issue for a long time.

I helped her to sit on the sofa and suggested she not speak anything. 'Please, Mumma, there is no use saying anything.'

Vinee apologised to my mother, attempting to assist her.

I said to my mother, 'Mumma, please understand why we are here. We need to take care of the family. We are not here so that you too suffer. I can't let this become a virus that affects everyone.'

Despite my efforts, the conflicts persisted. With so much quarrelling, I decided it was best for my mother to return to Mumbai. I didn't want her to endure such stress. After a week in Lucknow, I accompanied my mother to the airport, and Sweety picked her up at the Mumbai airport.

I had promised myself that I would handle the situation. I hired a maid to cook healthy meals and manage other responsibilities and expenses.

Chapter 15

The Collapse of Trust

My father-in-law was discharged from the hospital soon after. The doctor stated that when the ribcage is fractured, there is no surgery but self-healing. He was advised to rest at home until fully recovered.

My role mostly involved shuttling between the hospital and home. Sometimes I carried my father-in-law, at times Vinee, and sometimes Roshni.

On the second day after my father-in-law's discharge, I broached the topic with Vinee. 'We need to take a loan for the delivery and future expenses related to the baby and taking care of you post-delivery. Let's take a loan against your fixed deposit.'

'Why a loan in my name? Why not yours?' Vinee asked, sounding irritated.

'Don't worry! I will pay the EMIs. We have to take the loan anyway. But if I take a loan from an outside source, the interest will be around 14-15%. If we take a loan from your fixed deposit account, we only have to pay interest of 3-4%. I have done the research; it's the best interest—'

'What if you don't pay the interest? Will I have to deal with it during such a difficult period?'

'What do you mean? Of course, I will pay it, Vinee.'

'Then why don't you get it in your name?'

'14-15% to 3-4% is a big saving! I am thinking about us—'

'If you were thinking about us, you would have the money for all this, you idiot. In such a state of my family, you only see money. You want to take all the money I have, right? You yourself have nothing, right?'

'First of all, I am not taking your money. I am suggesting we can go for a loan on your FD that can provide a low-interest loan, which I will pay. Secondly, what is this, 'your money, my money?' Isn't it '*our* money'? I never said it was my money when I was spending it. And if I pay 14% interest, isn't our money spent extra?' I explained.

A small request turned into a big argument. She started shouting so loudly that my father-in-law entered the room.

'Don't worry about that; we will handle it,' he said.

'Papa, why would you take care of that? It is my responsibility, and I will do it,' I insisted.

'If she was your responsibility, you would have taken care of her in Mumbai, not here.'

'Papa, it was she who forced the decision of being here.'

'Don't make excuses now. It's as much your fault as it is hers.'

'Arpit,' Vinee screamed, 'You are bloody good for nothing.'

I looked at her father, hoping for some support. Instead, he stepped towards his daughter and started consoling her, giving me a deadly look. Rather than helping her understand, her father pointed fingers at me. Vinee began to abuse me in front of her father, even showing me her middle finger. I was perturbed that her father wouldn't stop her. When her father also raised his voice against me, I left the room, avoiding anymore drama.

I had a flight to Indore for work and a plan to return to Mumbai to check on my parents before heading back to Lucknow for the final days of Vinee's pregnancy. Before leaving, I requested my father-in-law to keep me updated and inform me if they needed anything.

'Yes, beta. Go,' he said. 'She is already stressed with the arguments. If you both are away, it will be better for the baby. But I will tell you when it is time.'

In a way, he was right. If Vinee and I were together, there would likely be unnecessary drama, impacting the baby. I wanted the last phase of her pregnancy to be stress-free, even if it meant sacrificing my immediate presence.

I departed with her father promising to take care of her and call me just before the delivery.

I was so stressed by the arguments that the moment I reached the airport, I blacked out and collapsed on the ground. A few people gathered and helped me, making me drink water.

'Are you okay? Do you want to call anyone?' a random stranger asked.

I washed my face, drank water, and called my father-in-law, who was the nearest person I knew around. However, his phone was not reachable. I dialled my sister in Mumbai, sharing the situation in my shaky voice.

'Connect me with any airport official, please, Arpit. I'll talk to them,' she requested.

The stranger overheard the conversation as the phone was on speaker, and he ran to call an airport official. I couldn't hear what my sister was telling the official, and my strong headache added to the difficulty.

A doctor arrived in a couple of minutes, taking me to an emergency room. They conducted my ECG, which showed a concerning report.

The doctor asked me if I had any stress.

'I … I,' Initially hesitant, trying to remember what and how it all happened, I expressed the entire situation to the doctor. I also told him about the blood I donated to my mother-in-law at the hospital. He warned me to take care of my body before taking care of others, as I myself was struggling.

'You are cleared to travel to Indore, but I suggest you should go to your hometown Mumbai, and see a doctor as soon as you land. This looks like something serious,' the doctor advised.

I cancelled my flight to Indore and booked the first flight to Mumbai, scheduled for the evening. After waiting for a couple of hours, I boarded the flight straight to Mumbai.

Upon reaching, I was so stressed that I didn't consider visiting the doctor.

'What should I do? I don't see things getting better. It is getting complicated day by day. How do I rectify this?' was all I could think.

I truly desired to find a way out of this daily stress and lead a good life.

In a relationship, when two people are angry or hurt, eventually, one has to let down their guard to save the relationship. However, it may raise concerns about losing self-respect, especially if it becomes a repetitive pattern.

Feeling troubled by these thoughts, I convinced myself one last time. With her due date approaching, I didn't want things to take a bad turn. I messaged her, urging her to set aside whatever happened and requesting her to calm down.

Her response shocked me.

She messaged that there was nothing left to talk about and instructed me not to message or call.

It made me wonder why she consistently wanted to break things instead of trying to fix them, even just once.

I called my father-in-law after 3 days and asked, 'I have booked a flight ticket on Friday. Is everything okay there?'

Her father shockingly replied, 'It's okay! I am handling things here. You don't have to come.'

'Papa, why shouldn't I? I have to be there. She is due any day now. I have my ticket booked too. I want to be there beside Mumma too.'

'Just cancel the ticket, Arpit. It's going to be the same if you come here. Both of you will argue, and she will be stressed. I can't afford that now.'

'Papa, but—'

'There are no ifs and buts here. I know what's good for the baby to come. Don't worry, beta, I am here, and I will let you know if I need you. I will call you when she is due.'

I couldn't reply much. I understood his point of view, no matter how desperately I wanted to be there.

I called Vinee, but she didn't pick up.

I messaged her, "I have talked to Papa. He wants me to be here in Mumbai and will let me know when to come. I had my ticket booked already, but couldn't push beyond his command. Vinee, please let me know if you have labor pain or any such trouble. I will reach there in 4-5 hours. Let me be with you."

But she didn't reply to my message either. Days passed by, but she didn't respond. I called Vinee and my father-in-law daily at least once. Vinee never responded, and my father-in-law called back very late, and at times didn't even call back.

I was anxious. I decided not to bother them, convincing myself that my father-in-law would call me when it was time.

I tried to focus on my work, understanding and accepting the situation.

A week later, I received a video call from Vinee. Although happy that she called, the content of the call left me with mixed emotions. She was in the hospital, holding a baby.

'Congratulations, Arpit. You are a father now. We have a baby boy,' she said.

Tears filled my eyes at the sight of the baby, but I felt a twinge of sadness for not being informed earlier, despite being repeatedly mentioned to come. My father-in-law's actions of not informing me were disheartening.

My immediate question was, 'At what time did we have the baby today?'

'It's his third day in this world. It was the day before yesterday,' Vinee said.

I was shocked. Looking at my parents, I saw they were equally stunned.

Why were we informed two days after the delivery?

While angry and sad, I controlled my emotions and told her, 'I will be there right away.'

Feeling upset that, as a father, I got to know after two days, we shared the good news with our relatives and friends. However, when they found out that it was already two days since the birth, reactions varied from unease to questions or laughter. We couldn't reveal that we were informed late. My parents made excuses, and everyone focused on the positive aspect of the news – Vinee and the baby being healthy. Deep down, though, we were awfully upset.

As soon as I reached Lucknow, I bought some things for the baby and Vinee. Having taken a cab to the hospital, I found out upon arrival that she had recently been discharged. Suppressing the thought of why she didn't inform me about this, I assumed they might have skipped it in stress.

Taking another cab, I reached home. My father-in-law had gone to visit my mother-in-law in the hospital. I was upset with Vinee, yet, when I entered the house, I asked her how she was, and then went into the room to see the baby.

'My baby,' I sighed, kissing my child. He was in a deep sleep at that point. Tears of happiness flowed from my eyes. It is a different feeling to hold your child in your hand. But at the same time, I felt bad that I was getting this opportunity two days late.

Vinee entered the room and observed us silently standing at the door. I couldn't look her in the eye for what she did. I carefully put the baby in the cradle and started telling Vinee about the things I had bought for them, bringing them out of my bag one after another.

She started crying and said, 'For two days, Arpit, I was all alone in the hospital. There was no one beside me. I was managing on my own.'

'But why? Papa said that he would manage it. He promised me that he would call me when it's time. I now feel foolish for trusting him,' I said. 'If he couldn't take care of you, he only had to tell me, which he promised but didn't do.'

My father-in-law had entered the house by then, listening to our conversation. I greeted him immediately as I saw him, but he didn't respond.

I was angry at him more than Vinee. I continued, 'I was expecting him to send me at least a message if he was busy enough to let me know.'

All of a sudden, Vinee started shouting at me. Her father too pounced on me, saying, 'This is why you are here? To argue and fight? This is why I didn't call you. I knew you would only make things tough for my daughter and her baby.'

'Papa, first of all, it is not me who raised the voice. You can clearly see the difference. And not her baby. It's my baby too.'

I don't know what they had in their mind. Both of them together started shouting at me.

I said, 'You guys don't know who are your well-wishers and who are against you. You are welcoming to the people who wish bad for you and throwing out people who wish good for you.'

They were going on and on. I stayed silent, kissed the baby, walked out of the room, took my belongings, wore my shoes, and left.

'Don't come again,' is what I heard from Vinee.

It was really difficult to deal with them.

I booked a hotel, instead of staying with them, waited for my flight, and left for Mumbai.

I decided that I wouldn't make the conversation until they understood who exactly was at fault. I wanted them to understand things and put their ego aside.

There was a family group of five siblings, the husbands of my sisters, Vinee, and my parents. Vinee used to share videos and images of our baby initially, and we would react to the videos.

On the other side, she didn't prefer to call or text me. I had to sacrifice one thing out of love and self-respect, and I chose to sacrifice my self-respect. I used to send messages on her stories, but she didn't respond to them either.

Then, out of the blue, a week later, she left the group.

It was a bit surprising for me as well, but I believed it was one of her angry sides that I had seen earlier.

The next day, I got a call from the Lucknow police station and I was shocked to know about the situation.

———❖❖———

Chapter 16

A Leap of Faith

Our first marriage anniversary was days away. So much had happened in the past year, with the biggest ups and downs. But the most beautiful thing that happened to us was becoming parents. We had a baby – one more reason why I wanted to save this relationship.

I started thinking of ways to fix the bond. I set aside my ego again and decided to surrender to hers, only to give our baby a better life.

So, I planned a surprise for them. I had my tickets booked for Lucknow a day before our anniversary. I started taking steps to resolve the issues between us, positively hoping that she would do the same.

We obviously couldn't go on a trip as our baby was hardly a month old. However, I had planned something special around our house in Lucknow. I searched for a restaurant, contacted the manager, and customised the hotel for that evening.

'When is the date, sir?' he asked on the call.

'6th December. But I will arrive there a day earlier and head straight to your restaurant to oversee the preparations. The day of the special dinner evening will be the 6th,' I said.

'Sure! I will order the materials and see what other things are needed.'

'Don't forget the photo-cake. I have just emailed you,' I said, checking my phone to confirm if the mail was sent.

'Received. We will start preparing. Waiting for your arrival, sir,' he said.

'Thanks,' I said and cut the call. I was really excited. I wanted to forget all the bad things that had happened in the past and start anew. I didn't want our baby to be raised in an unhappy space. I wanted to give Vinee and our baby all the happiness in the world.

However, on the day of our flight, when I went out to get some things for home, my scooter slipped on the road, and I had a minor accident. People gathered around until I came to my senses. I could feel the pain in my shoulders and arms.

One of them helped me get to a hospital. The doctor treated me, saying, 'Your left shoulder is dislocated. It's not that serious, but you need to be on bed rest for days.'

'But, madam, I have a flight to Lucknow.'

'When is it?'

'In the evening today.'

'No, Arpit, you can't. You are advised to take a rest. Forget Lucknow; you can't step outside of your house for almost two weeks.'

'Madam, but it's important.'

'I suggest not. It will be the worst. It should be a complete bed rest,' she said as if a teacher commanding her student.

She left the room, taking away my hopes of mending things with my partner this anniversary.

I called the manager of the restaurant and requested to shift our plan to the next week. He was hesitant at first, but when he heard about the accident, he suggested a date that would be unoccupied. I instantly cancelled my flight and booked a new flight ticket for the rescheduled date.

I guess life was becoming common for two things now—one, me cancelling a flight ticket, and two, my life giving me shocks right after I decided to fix things.

On that hospital bed, lying and looking at the ceiling, thinking about the challenges in my life, I had no idea that life had the biggest challenge ready for me the next day. Vinee had filed a complaint against me in Mahila Thana.

The woman on the call said, 'I am speaking from Mahila Thana, Lucknow. Your wife has filed a complaint against you that you have beaten her and asked for dowry. Since she couldn't pay, you sent her back to her parents' house.'

I was shocked to the core!

How on earth can she lie about it? What is this? Is it a fake call? Am I being pranked?

When I understood that this was something serious, I gathered my senses and spoke, 'It's a false complaint, madam. Nothing of such has happened.'

'We don't know all that. You have to come here and talk. We have to talk to you both together here.'

'I'll have to talk to my lawyer. Also, I have suffered an accident, so I can't be there for at least—'

She cut me off mid-sentence, saying, 'Yes, yes! We know people have accidents during this time only. I have seen a lot of people like you. Talk to whomever you want, just be here sooner than something worse happens to you and your family.' She cut the call, not letting me speak further.

I was so shocked that I lost my senses. Out of all the worst things, this is something that I never had imagined.

How could Vinee do this? Did she do it on purpose, or was she forced?

I got outside my home right away and started taking a senseless walk. I didn't know what was going on around me. I didn't know what was going on inside me. I was simply walking. I didn't care about my left hand being fractured and braced. I couldn't feel a part of my body.

All of a sudden, the children playing the game of cricket, the vendors shouting the price of vegetables, cars honking, and birds chirping, I could hear everything but couldn't sense it. It was as if someone had taken a big piece of my heart out. I was walking and walking, not knowing where to go and how to stop. My mind was consumed by the thoughts of what I heard and nothing else.

I was actually not in the present. The road was so busy that anything could have hit me. In fact, I crashed with some people, and they hurled abuses at me, and I didn't respond to that either. I ignored them and continued my walk with my mind playing it all over and over again.

There came a time when I was not even familiar with the roads and yet I was crossing the streets and walking aimlessly.

I was a lost traveller with no destination in mind.

When I got back to my senses, I realised that I had walked for more than seven kilometres.

I immediately called my lawyer and elaborated on my situation to him.

'Arpit, now listen to me *very carefully*,' he said, 'There is no solution to fix things with her now. If not for yourself, you need to think about your parents. This has escalated already. You have to file for divorce here in Mumbai before she files an official complaint. Because once she files an F.I.R., your family will be in big trouble. You and your parents will have to go to jail for a while. It can turn worse from here.'

'I don't think Vinee can be so bad to do this,' I said.

'We neither could think that she could put a formal complaint against you. It's okay if you can't accept completely what has happened, but don't let this spoil the lives of your family. I have seen such cases destroy lives,' he said.

In a way, he was right. I won't accept the thought that Vinee would destroy us, but she had already started it by complaining against me and my family, with false accusations.

'Police will have to take action if it turns into an F.I.R. It's a non-bailable offense. It will be better if you file for the divorce right away. If Lucknow police come to your door, you can show the filing of your divorce. We can say that the matter is in the court. They won't be able to arrest you or your family until the hearing date from the court,' the lawyer said.

Even though I couldn't understand what was happening, his words made sense. I had to be prepared for the worst. I didn't want my aged parents to face the trauma.

There might be a lot of men and women who can relate to this. Some of us have the capacity to fight to save the relationship until the very end of our lives. We don't give up on relationships that easily. We don't care if the other person might destroy us emotionally or legally. We still try to convince them, even if it means putting our self-respect on the line. We hold onto the relationship, hoping things will get better, even when it hurts us deeply. It is hard to let go because you believe so strongly in saving a bond. You know that sometimes holding on can cause more pain than letting go. Yet, you can't.

But when your partner wants to bring down your parents with you, that's when you have to give up on them. It's one thing to endure pain for the sake of love, but it's another to watch your loved ones suffer because of it. At that point, you realise that some sacrifices are too great, and some lines shouldn't be crossed. Letting go becomes necessary for the sake of those who truly care for you.

I filed for the divorce as per his suggestion, but I requested my lawyer not to send the notice to Vinee. I still wanted to find ways to talk to her and find a solution.

'Things might come back on track,' I said.

'I understand where you are coming from, Arpit. But even you and I know that things would never be on track after what she has done. She could have talked to you before doing all this. Anyway, if you want to give it a try, go for it. I won't send her any notice as of now,' he said.

I called the officer again and told her exactly what my lawyer had told me to say. I sent her my accident reports too. She scheduled the date three weeks from that day.

Vinee and I would be face-to-face again but in a completely different circumstance.

Till that date, it was the most difficult flight for me. I have always taken flights with excitement and energy, but that flight was quite the opposite.

I reached Lucknow on the scheduled date. However, upon reaching the Mahila Thana, I got to know that my date was rescheduled two days later, which I was not informed about. I signed on the register, clearly stating that I was present at the given time. I had a return flight the next day, so I stayed in a hotel and returned as per schedule.

On the very next day, I got a call from the department, saying, 'You were supposed to be here? Where are you?'

'I was there two days back, madam,' I said.

'Your date is today. You know what it means if you are absent on a given day?'

'I was not informed that my date is rescheduled. I was present there on my given day, and, in fact, have signed on the register.'

She took a while, probably checking the register, and said, 'Yes! The inspector handling your case is assigned to another role, and your case is now with another inspector. You have to be here today.'

'I stay in Mumbai. How can I be there today? And, I have no information about this rescheduling. I was there on my given date all the way from Mumbai. I talked to the SHO there, signed on the register, took her permission, and then left the place. If you expect me to be there right away, then it's not possible, madam,' I said.

She finally understood my position—why so late—and rescheduled a date three weeks later.

For three weeks, I was thinking about how and what to say to Vinee. I wanted her to take this all back and be with me on this journey of making our lives better. I somehow believed that things would get sorted out when we would sit together and discuss. Not even for once had I thought to break this relationship apart.

As per the date, I was present at the Mahila Thana in Lucknow. I was sitting, waiting for Vinee to come, so I could talk to her. However, when she arrived, she started crying loudly. I was dumbstruck by her reaction. She was behaving in such a way that it seemed as if I had done all that she had complained against me. I had seen Vinee in different avatars, but that avatar was heartbreaking for me.

On the other side, I had gone there with an album of our happy pictures together. I wanted Vinee to see and realise how happy we were, and also make the inspector see and decide if I truly did what Vinee blamed me for.

Along with the pictures, I attached all the financial transactions that happened between us – date and month-wise. I had gone with all the proofs. It was my lawyer's idea to prepare that book, which would save my family from humiliation if things escalated. It was a counter to whatever allegations she had put on me.

The book had the proof that the day she allegedly said that I had beaten her was the day when we were actually enjoying at Cafechino, the café in Multai. We were having a happy time together. I had pictures with my in-laws which clearly showed nothing of what Vinee said.

There were pictures of Vinee and me after our wedding, which included our honeymoon pictures of Goa as well.

Whatever she had mentioned in the complaint, I had the counters for it with evidence of photographs and screenshots. If only the inspector had seen the pictures, she would have realised that there is not even a percent of truth in what Vinee has said. Unfortunately, the officer did not even have a look at the book. She was talking to me in a very rude manner.

'I have seen guys like you a lot,' she said, angrily looking at me, consoling Vinee.

It is sad how the law system is inclined towards women. We promote equality and talk about how women should be given a position equal to men in every field, but we overlook the emotions of men. Why wouldn't they listen to the perspective of a man?

If a man complaints against a woman, she is innocent until proven guilty. But if a woman complains against a man, then he is guilty until proven innocent.

A man will be proved a criminal in the eyes of society until the court proves him innocent. It takes a woman to speak to be truthful, but a man has to bring evidence to be truthful. It is always men who would be the villain in everyone's eyes.

The manner in which the officer spoke was so rude that I called my uncle, the husband of my father's sister, who had served as a D.I.G. in Uttar Pradesh. He told the officer, 'See, we belong to a reputed family. There has never been a case like this in our entire family. All that you are seeing is not the truth. I request you to kindly go with the procedure and follow the evidence. Arpit has brought the proofs too. Please have a look at it. Just refer to it once, and on the basis of evidence, make your judgments.'

The officer gave a nervous smile, expressing her discomfort yet she had to do what she had to do. Uncle told me on call, 'Law has always been this way, Arpit. Even the police can't do anything. If a woman files an F.I.R. against her husband, they will have to take action. She has told me that she will refer your matter to the Family Court, and they will take forward this case. Based on the court's order and the report of the counselling session, they will take further action. Be very cautious with your wife. Don't do anything stupid that harms your family. You are still on the safe side in court.'

'Thanks, uncle. Really! I'll call you right after leaving,' I said, cutting the call.

The matter had moved to the court. Fortunately, I had listened to my lawyer and uncle, or else, this would have been far worse, looking at what Vinee had spoken against me. I could have been in jail, beaten behind bars, and my family would also have had to face embarrassment.

Thankfully, none of this happened since I used the advice of the right people around.

However, I still wanted to find a way to talk to Vinee and try to mend things up. There was a part of me wanting to fix the problems and lead a happy life together.

I was shaken up by how Vinee was crying, behaving like a victim inside the counselling room, and the moment she would come out, she would be all smiles. I was blown up by her behaviour. It was a rude awakening.

What a fine actress!

She would be absolutely normal outside. She would laugh on the phone, and speak smilingly with her lawyer. And the moment we would go inside the courtroom, I would see a different avatar. It was as if she had faced problems in our marriage. That was the first time I realised that I was married to a criminal. Only a criminal could change behaviour so immediately. That was the moment a lot of realisations hit me.

However, a part of me that wanted to save the relationship, come what may, would not die down. I had a couple of reasons – the baby, the fact that Vinee was the mother of my kid, and I wanted our baby to be raised with both her parents together.

I have to make her understand whatever she is doing is not good for the kid's future, I thought.

I made multiple calls to her and sent messages. She wouldn't answer any of them. I even started sending her emails, but those too remained unanswered. Come rain or shine, I just wanted to share all my feelings with her. It was one of those moments when the desire for mutual understanding was so strong that the only way to achieve it was by pouring your heart out with words. I wanted her to know what I felt and what I truly wished for us. Maybe, just maybe, she would change her mind. Maybe, just maybe, something would trigger her, and at the very least, she would have a heart-to-heart conversation with me.

I thought that if we could just have one heart-to-heart conversation, we might finally reach a consensus.

For almost a year, between the court dates, I did the same. I tried to communicate with her, wanting to change things but had the same result. She kept on ignoring me.

For once she replied to me, saying, "You and your family have troubled me a lot. I have had enough!"

It sounded like she messaged back just for the sake of collecting some evidence. She had made up her mind that she didn't want to fix things between us. All she wanted was a divorce with a big settlement amount.

In all this process, although slowly, I had convinced myself of what she truly wanted, and there was no way to bring us together. It was almost a year that my calls, messages, and emails were being ignored.

I had started accepting the reality.

Chapter 17

The Battle Beyond the Courtroom

A year had passed, and it was the first birthday of our kid. I had sent gifts which she sent me back unopened. It was sad how she wouldn't let me reach my kid too. I had learned to control myself not to call her or try to reach her to make her understand. However, whenever we used to meet in court, I would lose all the strong-layers, and once again be the man who was emotionally attached to her. My weeks and weeks of control would be shattered to pieces in that instance when I would see her.

The same thing happened when we were meeting after three months in court. The moment I saw her, I initiated conversations, and she would ignore me.

I and my lawyer discussed how our case was getting weak in Family Court, and we decided to challenge the decision in the High Court in Lucknow. Generally, high courts don't take family matters, but luckily, based on my evidence, they accepted my appeal.

On the first day of the hearing in the High Court, Vinee didn't come. I was the only one there. The court warned her and ordered her to be present at the next hearing. They heard our matter from both perspectives and suggested in-house counselling.

Again, the series of counselling sessions started. I would travel alone from Mumbai to Lucknow, not wanting to trouble my family. She would either come with her father or with a friend.

As usual, inside the counselling room, she would act and cry in front of the counsellor with her common complaints – how they tortured me and all – with no evidence, and step out of the room acting normal.

However, the one who was handling our sessions in High Court was a very experienced counsellor. He understood in the first meeting itself what's the truth. He knew who was right and who was wrong. After a couple of counselling sessions, He instructed us, 'Arpit, Vinee, bring your parents with you next time. We would want to hear their perspective.'

That was the first time in the process that my parents had to travel to Lucknow with me. She had brought her parents as well. It was all the same for me, cold-hearted and hurt until I saw my kid. A family man in me woke up! When I took the kid in my arms, I was literally in tears.

There is a room for kids in the High Court, where parents can keep the baby and make them eat and drink. There are toys as well for the kids to play with.

In that room, Vinee was behaving very nicely to me, saying, 'Our kid likes this toy. He is more comfortable sleeping on his right. When he yawns, he just looks like you.'

She shared soothing things in the room, making me see how things could be if it were normal. Just when I imagined that short-lived normal to be true, she would show her true colours.

The moment we stepped out of the room, I asked her, 'When did he start to walk?'

It was a general question, to which she replied irritably, 'As a father, you don't even know that? What father would you have been? How the hell would you share the responsibility of a father when you don't know when a baby starts to walk?'

I was thinking that only 30 seconds earlier, when we were inside the kids' room, she would talk to me politely, and now that we were open, in front of our family and lawyers, she would start getting angry at me.

Why such a drastic change of behaviour? It clearly showed that she wanted to portray herself as a victim who was tortured and left alone to raise a baby. That was the moment I was out of my mind completely. She was now getting out of my heart and I didn't want to try save the relationship anymore.

When in the counselling room, she first time clearly spoke that she wanted a divorce. 'I want my maintenance as well as my kid's maintenance,' she said. 'I don't want to live with this man.'

I realised that day that chasing her was of no use. She had really made up her mind and was so clear about what she wanted.

Post that session, I used to be there not as a husband to her, but as a human wanting to end this and find myself. I had lost so much in myself that instead of my previous focus on saving the relationship, I wanted to save what was broken in me.

In the High Court, our settlement letter was made. She had initially demanded 1 crore and 7 lakh rupees (10.7 Million Rupees). But since the counsellor had understood who was right and who was wrong, she told us, her gaze on Vinee, 'See, there are two things. Either you can destroy each other's lives or think about your future. Arpit clearly can't give you that much of an amount. He will fight in court. And there, in front of the judge, the fight would be on the basis of evidence. Court won't see if you are a man or a woman, only evidence would talk.'

The counsellor's words triggered fear in Vinee. I could sense her petrified inside out. She knew she had no evidence to prove her allegations, while I had everything that proved whatever she was saying was wrong.

How would she generate messages or voice recordings of dowry or even present a witness for it when we hadn't asked dowry from her? How would she get pictures of her bruises or get a witness of it when I had never raised my hands on her? How would she get evidence of us removing her from our house when nothing of that had happened?

She knew that fake evidence would be caught, and she would be punished for it. There was no other way for her than approaching mutual settlement.

She demanded 15 lakhs, and I started with 1 lakh. We both concluded on 6 lakhs, and the settlement letter was made. I gave her 3 lakhs in a few days while the other 3 lakhs were supposed to be given after the final signature.

On the basis of the settlement letter made in the High Court, we applied for divorce in the Family Court. On the first hearing, she made a lot of drama to edit things on paper. She wanted to state that she could get married whenever she wanted after the divorce, the baby would be staying with her, and she would have his custody for life. She also wanted to state that I could meet the kid only once a year. But I objected and corrected that I could meet my kid every 2 months. The court gave me permission for the same.

It had already been 19 months since she had filed a complaint against me. In these months, my life went upside down. I saw a police station and a court. I traveled from Mumbai to Lucknow and back multiple times. We had our disputes in the Family Court. I challenged the decision in the High Court. With the settlement, the travel, arranging money, and managing things, I had faced a hell lot of stress.

I was standing tall, ensuring that I fought it out alone, not letting my parents get involved in the police and court visits. Because it was my decision to get married, my family should not bear any problems.

But in this process of fighting on my own, my mind and body had taken a toll. We still had two hearings left for the divorce. I was very depressed and heartbroken about what had happened in my life.

Right after the second hearing—after the settlement order from the High Court—my health was deteriorating. I was not able to walk for more than ten steps. I used to feel exhausted and would blackout many times. I had pain in my chest and would sweat every now and then. It wasn't normal, and I knew there was something off.

Chapter 18

A Chance to Live

I realised that I was constantly traveling. I traveled from Mumbai to Lucknow for the court hearing, and I had this feeling in me that there was some problem since I was having an issue walking even a few steps. I had chest pain and discomfort that kept coming back.

After the hearing, I went straight to Bangalore from Lucknow for work purposes. It was during this trip that the pain in my chest escalated. I was not able to walk even a bit.

As my company is in the cardiac division, the CEO, who is also a cardiologist, quickly suggested after hearing my situation, "Arpit, there is something wrong. Please stay back in Bangalore and come to my hospital. And if there is anything serious, I will personally perform your surgery."

Everyone was under the impression it would be angioplasty, a procedure to open narrowed or blocked blood vessels that supply blood to the heart. No one had in mind that it would be one of the complicated surgeries that would change the tracks and wacks of my life.

Considering my condition, I was mentally prepared for the surgery. But then I told my CEO, "Let me just go to Mumbai. If it's surgery, I need my family around to take care of me afterward."

"Okay, that's fair. But as soon as you reach, please go and get yourself tested," he said.

The flight to my hometown was tough. I felt confused about what would happen next. Life never stopped throwing challenges my way, and I was doing my best to face them all. But amidst it all, I knew one thing for sure – if I could overcome these problems, something better was waiting for me.

"It's all part of God's plan to make me stronger," I reminded myself.

When I reached Mumbai, I called the same surgeon who had treated my father. He asked me to come down to the hospital, and I was there sooner. He looked at my old reports, which were done a year earlier than that day. There was an error, and the doctor had missed telling me about it. It was a case of medical negligence.

Now, the new doctor saw the report and said, "Arpit, why didn't you take any action? Clearly, there is a problem in your last year's reports, and you should have taken action then."

I told him, "The doctor who had my tests done never told me about the issue."

The next day, I went for the angiography, a type of X-ray used to check blood vessels, where you exactly get to know about your blockages. My sisters were with me when the angiography was done.

I remember when the doctor was performing my angiography, I was looking at his face. Somewhere I got this feeling that there is a bigger problem.

But … it was the reports that shocked us.

"Multiple arteries are blocked," the doctor told my sister, "Even veins are blocked. The only option is to go for bypass surgery."

My sisters were extremely shocked to hear that. One of them came towards me, and she caressed my head. I immediately understood that there was something critical.

I asked my sister at that moment, "Did the doctor ask for a bypass surgery?"

She didn't reply.

I asked her again, and that's when she replied in a very heavy voice, as she had cried after hearing it from the doctor, "Yes, the doctor has suggested going for bypass surgery. That is the only option. You have multiple blocked arteries."

I wanted to see how severe it is. The surgeon came to my ward and started explaining to me, and how important it is to get the bypass surgery done on an immediate basis.

Somewhere, I was mentally unprepared because there was one thing constantly running in my mind. I was only 37 years old and if I went for bypass surgery, what would my life look like after that surgery?

What if something happens to me?

I was concerned about that.

I was also hesitant to go for surgery, which would leave marks on my body. But the CEO of my company from Bangalore called me. He explained to me in a very clinical term how important it is to go for bypass surgery right now, looking at my situation.

Also, my reporting manager, who is based in Mumbai, came to the hospital and explained it to me in very technical terms. He also assured me that my life would be better than my current life health-wise.

Listening to them, I felt comforted to some extent. I was trying to mentally prepare myself.

Yet, I told my doctor, "I want to go back home and think it over for a couple of days and then come back."

My surgeon told me, "Arpit, I won't stop you from going back home. But let me tell you that I'll be very unhappy if you go back because looking at your situation we really don't have time. It is better that you go for the surgery tomorrow. I can assure you that things will go back to normal soon. You will be able to walk, run, and cycle. You will be able to do all those things you desire to do. Your physical health will significantly improve after surgery. But post-surgery, there should be rest for a couple of days, and you have to look after a few things for a couple of months. It's just a matter of 3 to 4 months maximum. And then you will be all good."

It was a tough decision to make!

My sister also realised that I was thinking over it too much. I said yes to the surgery considering their advice on the very next day. She called my school friends, Aman and Karan. They came to the hospital and started cheering me up. They helped me divert my mind from the stress and I felt relaxed around them.

Have you ever faced a surgery?

That feeling. It is like stepping into a world where time slows down and every heartbeat feels magnified.

You find yourself on a hospital bed, surrounded by the sterile scent of antiseptic and the hushed voices of nurses and doctors full of activity around you.

There is uncertainty in the room, with a strange mix of fear and hope.

Your mind races with questions – Will everything go smoothly? Will I wake up feeling whole again?

It is a moment of vulnerability unlike any other, where you place your trust in the hands of strangers who hold your life in their grasp.

And as the anaesthesia takes hold and the world fades into darkness, you are left with nothing but faith that you will emerge on the other side, changed but alive.

It was that feeling for me.

On the day of the surgery, a few assistant doctors and nurses came to my ward to get me to the operating theatre. They gave me a red-colored liquid to apply to my entire body and then take a shower. When I was applying that liquid to my body, I got this feeling that I was about to die now.

That was the first time I felt, "What if I die?"

It was a very different feeling, and I had never felt that before. But at a certain moment, I felt very relaxed because I had no regrets.

Before the surgery, one has to sign a form stating that if anything happens to you in the operating theatre, the doctor is not responsible.

Bypass surgery is one of the most complicated surgeries. It was but obvious to have this feeling of "What if… What if something happens to me in the operating theatre?"

When I was being taken to the operating theatre on a stretcher, I saw all my sisters around me. I saw all my friends. They started taking my pictures. I smiled in front of the camera. This was something that I felt within as well as I was ready for it.

It was not a normal operation, but bypass surgery. My life was at risk. Strangely, unlike most people who would panic, I remained in control of my senses. I strongly believed that things would turn out for the best.

In the operating theatre, I was laid down, and I could see the LED lights focusing on me. When one of the nurses was giving me anaesthesia, the surgeon told me, "Arpit, I am putting you to sleep. I'm very sure that you will do well."

I raised my thumb, and that's it. I was put to sleep. I was completely unconscious.

Slowly I got back to my senses. It took me over a minute to realise that I was alive.

I still remember waking up outside of that operating theatre. They were transferring me from the operating theatre to the ICCU (intensive critical care unit). That is where patients are supposed to be after the surgery.

Because of the anaesthesia, I was still hallucinating. I had a blurry image of Karan and Aman and one of my sisters. She was standing there, holding my hand.

From the stretcher, I was transferred onto the bed. Post-surgery, there are a lot of fluids that form in your body. These are bad fluids that need to be drained out of your body. There were drains on my groin and stomach, here and there.

I had a very blurry image of my sister, and that's when I asked her, "What time is it?"

She told me, "It's 12."

I did the calculation. The wards had come around 7:45 AM to take me to the operating theatre. So when she told me 12, I thought it was 12 in the afternoon.

I asked her, "Did you have your lunch?"

She said, "Arpit, it's 12 at night."

That's when it hit me!

I asked her, "How many hours did my surgery go on?"

"Almost 11 hours."

I was shocked, "How bad was the surgery?"

"Your three arteries were completely blocked. There were veins which are blocked too. So there were four grafts that were supposed to be done."

At the age of 71, my father had three grafts. And for me, it was four.

There were four bypasses that were done!

Listening to that, I was completely blown. I had my birthday seven days after my surgery, so I had that goal in my mind to kind of make sure that I remained mentally strong.

Come what may, I want to celebrate this birthday at home! I told myself.

I didn't want to celebrate my birthday in the hospital. That was my primary goal.

I used to lay on the bed the entire day, which was obvious. There were multiple thoughts running through my mind. There were negative thoughts too, but I used to quickly push them away and let the positive ones stay.

All through, it was really boring for me. But I kept my mind busy. I used to think about my parents and sisters. I used to think about how I was alive.

I started practicing the art of gratitude.

That slowly and gradually pushed away all the negative thoughts. I became mentally strong during my stay in the hospital with a positive attitude.

The moment I was out of the ICCU and brought to the ICU, I tried to do things on my own. I tried to get up myself, taking precautions. I tried to go to the washroom myself.

This determination was inspired by a principle I had learned during my days at Tech Mahindra, a Japanese strategy called Kaizen. Kaizen emphasises gradual, continuous improvement and the willingness to make small, daily advancements rather than seeking a major overhaul. This approach taught me to focus on steady, incremental progress, which became a guiding force in my recovery journey.

When the physiotherapist came in the afternoon, she took me to the hallway, and I made sure that I walked twice through the entire hallway on my own. Seeing this, even the physiotherapist gave positive feedback to my surgeon, "He is recovering well. If we give him an exercise, he makes sure that he repeats those exercises twice or thrice."

As a result, I was discharged on the afternoon of my birthday and celebrated the day at home in the presence of my family and friends. That was the time I realised that I was not as mentally weak as I used to think.

I cherished this strength of mine.

Post my surgery, I began my self-development journey. I began watching a lot of positive YouTube content. Then I started creating content myself and educated people. I spoke about body alarms and taking massive actions upfront.

When I look back at my life, I realise that the difficult moments I faced were actually blessings in disguise. They have taught me valuable lessons and helped me grow into a stronger and wiser person. I am grateful for every obstacle I encountered because they pushed me to become better.

I understand that many people are going through tough times right now, and it can feel difficult. But it is important to remember that challenges are temporary. They may seem insurmountable at the moment, but with perseverance, you can overcome them.

The fact is that the hurdles you conquer add to your strength and prepare you for whatever lies ahead.

So, don't lose hope. Keep moving forward, and trust that you have the strength within you to weather any storm.

—◆◆—

Chapter 19

The Power of Forgiveness

I had won a battle, but it was time for me to end the war I had been fighting for long and move on.

I was supposed to pay six lakh rupees to Vinee for the settlement, out of which I already paid three lakhs to her. But then this bypass surgery happened, and there were a lot of expenses involved.

Luckily, my salary was not deducted even though I was not at work – a fantastic support that I received from my company. I used to get my full salary on time when I was fighting in court and lying in a hospital bed.

That helped me to save some money.

Before my last hearing, I paid the balance amount to Vinee. On the basis of the demand draft, the judge approved the divorce.

On that particular day, I was expecting her to be humble by then. I was expecting her to say, "This is the last day. Let's wish each other well and move on towards our respective lives."

However, her behaviour was completely opposite.

The judge had asked me for five lakh rupees of health insurance for my kid, which I did at my last hearing. I had forwarded the document to Vinee. I'm not sure if she really missed having a look at it or just wanted to create some ruckus.

She said that she never received the health insurance document.

I said, "I had already forwarded it to you via email and WhatsApp."

She claimed that she never received it.

There, in court, I had to dig through my files and find the digital copy of the insurance. I forwarded it to her then and there.

In front of the judge, she argued, "Why is your name mentioned after my kid? Why is it, Yashraj Arpit Upadhyay? It should only be 'Yashraj'. I will not accept this."

"For you, the most important thing is, God forbid, if there is a need for him to get hospitalised, whether the document will be utilised or not. It doesn't matter if my name is there or not, but the document will be used.

That is what matters. And it is not in my control to print the name. The insurance company does it," I said.

She argued, "No! Let us take the next date. Get the policy renamed and give it to me."

Then finally, her lawyer convinced her, "Let's not create an issue now. It is legal, and let's go ahead and get this done."

Vinee accepted the document, signed it, and we got divorced.

I had a flight back to Mumbai, so I chose to be at the airport rather than a hotel. I went to a café at the airport, ordered a coffee, and started thinking about the last two years of my life. So much had happened: my second marriage, my father's bypass surgery, the everyday hustle of managing my relationship with Vinee, Vinee's pregnancy, Vinee's parents' accident, my shoulder dislocation, my own bypass surgery, trips to the police station and court, my kid, and finally, the divorce. It all came as flashes. So much had happened in just two years, and it had changed me as a person.

In fact, my life had changed for the better. I sensed this calmness within me, and I felt happiness.

When I came back, I had a goal in my mind that I wanted to achieve.

I started creating content on narcissism, loneliness, and how a person is never ready for life after divorce or separation. I also focused on the importance of keeping your mind sane and maintaining hope while going through these hardships. Finding the balance, or the TAO, between the extremes became essential for me. I realised that I was actually with a narcissist, and sharing my experiences could help others facing similar struggles.

This is a very big subject in itself, and I have a written documentary on these topics!

When you are in a relationship with a narcissist, the only thing you can do, if you decide to stay with them, is to manage your relationship.

I read a fantastic book regarding this subject – "Should I Stay Or Should I Go: Surviving A Relationship With A Narcissist" by Dr. Ramani Durvasula.

I started researching on the same topic - what is narcissism and how to identify a narcissist around you – and created content on that.

A narcissist is one such personality type of humans, which is different from all the other personality types. A narcissist can never change in their life. If you decide to stay with them, as I said earlier, all you have to do is learn to manage your relationship with them.

I felt I was in a phase of life where I wanted to help those people who have gone through a similar pattern of life. That emptiness that I used to feel within me, that pain that I used to feel during the time of my divorce, I really wanted to help those people convert this feeling into the feeling that I have today.

I have been there. I know what it feels like. I used to lie down in bed for hours and hours and scroll through my mobile screen. I used to feel numb. Emptiness had crawled upon me and darkness had turned to be my home. I didn't know the way to come out of it. Or rather I say, I didn't want to come out of it. It took me a lot of time to gather myself and decide to get my way out.

Even though I was alive, I was mentally dead.

I used to look at the fan and ceiling and wall and mobile screen for hours with no thoughts running in my mind.

I was a living dead!

For a moment, I used to laugh, and suddenly, the next moment, I would cry. An emotional video would turn me over emotional. A stand-up comedy video would make me laugh out loud. I couldn't control my emotions. In fact, my emotions used to control me.

And this is something an individual faces at least once in his or her life. No matter what the reason is – be it personal or professional.

After a few months in this state, a mental alarm suddenly went off in my mind. I realized I was in deep trouble. Standing before the mirror that day, I introspected: Why am I doing this? Is this truly helping me? I understood then that I had two choices: either blame fate or find the good in this situation and grow from it. I chose the latter.

During this phase, I learned about different energies and how to unblock them. It's ironic that the importance of these energies is never taught in our schools and colleges. In ancient Indian times, there was a system of guru (spiritual teacher) and shishya (a pupil of a guru). Today, however, we identify ourselves as intellectual beings only when we excel academically.

Today, I feel more aware of myself. I feel more connected to my inner self. I don't need any external motivation to be joyful. I don't feel the need to watch a stand-up comedy show to laugh. I am a self-motivated person, and I have regained my lost joy.

I feel like a child who doesn't need any external sources to be joyful. If you bring a child a toy or act in front of them, the child will enjoy it. They don't need any motivation to be happy or laugh; a small act will make them joyful. This is because they don't have any energy blocks, and I can feel the same cheer within me.

I got a sense of purpose here that there must be so many people in this world who must be going through a similar phase of life I have already started walking on the journey to make sure I equip myself and learn those skills to help people.

I felt like helping those sets of people to come out of the emptiness that I felt once.

It was like an alarm in my life regarding the problem I had come out of. I knew that there would be people struggling with the same feeling and I got the purpose in me to transform their life like I did with my life.

I started realising that I was not the problem. The problem lay with the other person. All the self-doubt and self-criticism were because of gaslighting—someone else making me feel that way deliberately.

All this while, when I was in a relationship with Vinee, there were a lot of things that I started questioning about myself. I started questioning my ability to talk and to work. Basically, I started questioning my being. There was this myth in my mind that I was good for nothing.

I was in a loop ... A loop of depression.

There were a few books that helped me. One of which is "Courage To Be Disliked" by Ichiro Kishimi and Fumitake Koga. For me, that book is all about how it's not the way you perceive the world. Your perception of the world can be negative or positive, but it completely depends on you and whether you change your perspective about the world.

That really helped me realise and understand that it was me who was perceiving myself as a negative person and a person who is good for nothing, only because someone else was constantly telling me that.

I started questioning myself, "Is that really true?"

That is when I started having a different perspective about myself. That was the first book that I read.

The second book that really helped me to be positive was "The Magic" by Rhonda Byrne. This book taught me to be grateful for what I have rather than thinking about all the negative things that happened to me.

This is also one of the books that helped me during my hospitalisation phase.

As I said, I was only focusing on the positive things that I have in my life with the loved ones around me, and "The Magic" was one of the books that helped me, which I read just before my surgery.

I would also re-mention the book "Should I Stay Or Should I Go," which is about narcissism. I learned about my ex-wife's behaviour and how I was dealing with a narcissist. That's when I started deleting all the episodes that happened to me.

With the help of this book, I also understood that it is not their fault that they are dealing with a unique personality type. This is the exact reason why I was not bothered by what happened to me in the past because I had learned about that particular human behaviour.

Next, I read "The 10X Rule" by Grant Cardone, which particularly taught me about how I can put 10X efforts into anything, and I would definitely get results.

I started putting 10X efforts into my work and my personal life and in whatever I was doing. As a result, I got an opportunity to become the Africa Head from the Zonal Manager. I used to take care of the western part of the country earlier, and then I became the Head of a Continent for my company.

I started focusing on my health and my diet. The relationships around me with my family and friends also improved because I started working on myself. I was far away from those negative thoughts that gave me nothing but self-doubt and self-criticism.

There is also a book which I read called "Can't Hurt Me" by David Goggins. It's the story of David who became a Navy SEAL despite having an extremely difficult childhood. He has mentioned the abuse from his father and how he and his mother left his father and then started living on their own. He mentioned the difficulties he faced in school and having a speech problem during his childhood for which he was bullied by his schoolmates. It is about how he overcame those challenges and became one of the greatest Navy SEALs.

This book really helped me to build mental toughness, embrace discomfort and pain, accountability and self-reflection, self-discipline, and hard work.

After the surgery, I developed a very strong mindset. I set a strong goal for July 27th, 2028, to help 1 million people going through similar challenges. I never want financial concerns to dictate my choices. I aim to have a stable source of income that covers my lifestyle and monthly needs, allowing me to focus on my mission and passions without worry.

Then, I can turn my journey towards traveling to multiple different places and helping people who are facing these challenges.

In today's world, there's a noticeable gap in human connection. One of the primary culprits behind this is our obsession with mobile phones. We're so engrossed in our screens that we've lost touch with the simple, yet profound, human interactions that bring warmth and meaning to our lives.

This has resulted in depression, with more and more people feeling lonely, feeling like they don't have anyone around them. People spend hours scrolling through social media, comparing their lives to others, and feeling inadequate. The lack of real, meaningful connections has made it hard for many to find support when they need it the most.

Loneliness often sneaks in quietly, for many different reasons. When someone has a serious illness, this loneliness makes their pain even worse. This often leads people to turn to their electronic devices for comfort. But these gadgets can only give temporary relief, not the deep support that real human connection offers. In our digital world, we need to remember the importance of human touch and real social support.

One must accept that in life, there is no substitute for genuine relationships between people. As the famous saying goes, the best thing about having a bad day is that it makes you appreciate the good ones that much more. Sometimes, instead of being glued to the screens of our devices, we should turn our phones off and interact with others. Nurturing close, positive affiliations enables us to feel less lonely and disconnected.

Loneliness can be overcome, and one way to do that is by reaching out and not being passive. I learned this during a tough time with Vinee. I thought disconnecting from everyone would bring me peace, but I didn't realise I wasn't mentally ready to handle it alone. This led me into a deep depression.

To beat loneliness, you should engage in real-life interactions and actively participate in your local community and social events. These connections can help rebuild broken relationships and ensure you don't feel isolated. Additionally, finding hobbies and activities you enjoy can lead to friendships with like-minded people, bringing happiness and a sense of belonging. If you are not motivated enough to do it yourself, find someone very close who can do it for you. For me, it was my friends and family.

Technology is good, but it can't substitute the feeling of holding someone in your arms, holding hands, or talking face-to-face. Thus, we must work to invest in a society where all people feel welcome and appreciated. This is also one of the reasons why we see people divorcing frequently today. It is often said that human beings are both the luckiest and unluckiest species on earth. They are lucky because they have choices, but unlucky because they have too many choices. In the current society, people are enticed to think that everything on the other side is always better than what they have. A lot of people are quick to throw in the towel when things get tough in their relationships, probably because of the many options that are out there.

Modern technology, especially social networks and dating sites, has made it easy to meet new people, and therefore we tend to neglect our present relationships.

Instead of working on conflict resolution and relationship enhancement, we might think about searching for new contacts at the first sight of a conflict. This never-ending quest for a better life can result in a cycle of discontent and insecurity.

However, this is deceptive because it presents perfect relationships in a way that sets the bar too high. Couples begin to gauge their own relationships against these high standards and are left dissatisfied. This makes them feel frustrated and even think their partner is not worthy of them, leading some to prefer divorce.

At the same time, it is essential to understand that real relationships involve time, commitment, and interaction. Every relationship has its problems, which can often be overcome, making the relationship between two people even stronger. Rather than getting distracted by the array of choices out there, we should emphasise the significance of the bonds we share.

When we pay attention to the effects of being overwhelmed with choices, we can come into our relationships with more appreciation and loyalty. We have to realise that happiness and self-satisfaction stem from the value we put in relationships over continuously chasing something fresh. This way, we can develop an even stronger bond that can effectively stand the challenges of everyday life.

The human touch and personal connections we once had before smartphones are now often missing. I want to help people regain this through a simple framework I call "RISE":

- R: Recognise your feelings.

- I: Identify what contributes to your loneliness.

- S: Strategise ways to overcome it.

- E: Embrace the bliss that follows.

R: Recognize Your Feelings

Take a moment to truly sit with your feelings of loneliness. Don't push them away or judge yourself for feeling this way. Instead, give yourself the grace to acknowledge those emotions. Reflect on what might be triggering them, and understand that it's okay to feel lonely—it's a part of the human experience.

I: Investigate the Cause

Dig a little deeper into what's contributing to your loneliness. Is it certain relationships? Old wounds that haven't healed? Or maybe the stories you've been telling yourself? Look at both your social surroundings and your inner thoughts. Sometimes, we need to understand where we are before we can figure out how to move forward.

S: Strategize Your Way Forward

Start small. Come up with simple, manageable actions that can help you connect with others. Maybe it's sending a message to a friend or signing up for a class you've always wanted to take. Don't worry about huge changes right away; focus on those first steps that will slowly bring more connection and joy into your life.

E: Embrace Your Bliss

Now, imagine what your life could look like when loneliness is no longer the defining feeling. Picture yourself living a life filled with connection, purpose, and joy. Set meaningful goals that resonate with who you are and what you love. Celebrate every little victory along the way, and remember to practice gratitude for the positive changes, no matter how small they may seem. You deserve a life of bliss.

Chapter 20

Uniting with the Self

I was back in India from Kenya for a solo trip to Ladakh.

"It's so good to see this adventurous side of you, Arpit," one of my sisters said on a video call earlier in the day.

"I am finding it amazing too. Just exploring this side of me, Soni," I replied.

Not only the adventurous side but in the past couple of years, I have seen a lot of new sides of me. After the storm, I felt my life turning brighter with each passing day.

Coming back to my Ladakh trip, I had this on my wish list, and as soon as I came back to Mumbai, I had planned this trip before going back to Kenya. I wanted to make it solo, although my friends insisted on joining, as I wanted to be with myself in what people call Heaven-on-Earth.

Standing atop a rocky outcrop in Ladakh, I took a deep breath, the fresh air filling my lungs. It was a place that held both the promise of adventure and the solace of solitude.

I was lost in my thoughts when a familiar voice came through, calling me from behind. "Arpit?"

I turned around and was surprised to see Kaushik approaching me with a warm smile on his face. I still remember, years ago, how we had a chance to meet each other on a train where I requested him to change seats and he instantly agreed.

We exchanged contacts and then shared our tickets to show to the TC. That allowed us to stay connected by viewing each other's WhatsApp stories and replying to them occasionally. I unknowingly found a friend that day, with whom I stayed connected digitally. And here we are, quite surprisingly, meeting each other again.

"Kaushik!" I said with a mixture of delight and disbelief. "What are you doing here?"

He shrugged nonchalantly. "Just exploring, like you, I suppose. Funny how life has a way of bringing people back together, isn't it?"

"Indeed, it is. And it seems we are both headed in the same direction. Care to join me?"

He nodded eagerly. We hired a bike soon and began our journey together. The miles passed in comfortable silence, broken only by sporadic conversation as we exchanged stories of our respective adventures since we last met.

Eventually, as we settled into a rhythm, Kaushik broached a topic. "So, Arpit. I couldn't help but notice that you are traveling alone this time. What happened to the woman you were with before on the train."

My expression softened, a wistful smile playing at the corners of my lips as I recalled the memories of my past. "Ah, yes. She was a part of my life for a time, but like all things, our paths diverged eventually. We shared some incredible moments together, though."

I told him my entire story and he listened to it very patiently.

He nodded in understanding, sensing the depth of emotion while taking time to gently ask, "And how do you feel now, being on your own?"

I looked at the distant horizon as I searched for the right words. "You know, Kaushik, I have come to realise that all that happened actually gave me the opportunity to rediscover myself in ways I never thought would be possible. I have learnt to embrace the uncertainty of life, to find joy in the journey itself."

"You have come a long way since we last met," he said.

"Indeed, I have. Life has a way of throwing us into unexpected situations, but I have learned to face them head-on, to embrace the challenges rather than shy away from them. I have discovered strengths within myself that I never knew existed."

"If you had the chance to go back in time and change things, would you?"

I shook my head, gave a smile, and said, "I wouldn't change a thing. Every experience, every setback, has shaped me into the person I am today. And for that, I am grateful."

❖